Laura Ashley, Inc.
6 St. James Avenue, 10th Floor, Boston, MA 02116

Presented on the Occasion
of
the Opening of the Laura Ashley
North American Headquarters
October 21, 1992

LAURA ASHLEY STYLE

LAURA ASHLEY STYLE

Iain Gale & Susan Irvine

Weidenfeld & Nicolson
LONDON

George Weidenfeld and Nicolson Limited
91 Clapham High Street
London SW4 7TA

ISBN 0 297 79057 9

Design concept by Mavis Henley

Colour separations by Newsele Litho Ltd
Filmset by Keyspools Ltd, Golborne, Lancashire
Printed and bound in Italy by LEGO, Vicenza

CONTENTS

FOREWORD

Laura Ashley style is epitomized for many by the tiny floral monoprints which have decorated many a Victorian-style bedroom, and with which the company first made its name. But as you will see from the following pages, this is just one strand of an ever-evolving story.

As a print house dedicated to reproducing the designs of bygone eras, Laura Ashley is deeply rooted in the history of art and design. We prefer to look to the past for inspiration, believing that designs that have been developed over the years have both timelessness and strength. Sections of this book are devoted to the history of design and decoration, a history that has been the inspiration for our designs – either as a direct influence or, just as significantly, as a catalyst sparking off new ideas and directions.

Yet while inspiration is taken from the past, Laura Ashley designs are very much a part of the present. Whether you choose to surround yourself with patterns and prints, or whether you prefer the simple elegance of plain colours, the desire is surely to create an atmosphere that is warm and welcoming – just as the bower bird creates an inviting arbour with brightly coloured pebbles and flowers. Creating the right atmosphere is fundamental to the decoration of one's home, and for Laura Ashley the key to achieving this is comfort, first and foremost. We believe that a well-designed home is created with function very much in mind. It should complement the lifestyle of the owners and encompass all the activities that will take place there. I suggest that this should be your starting point. Whether your priorities are family, animals and health, the arts, fun or fantasy, design your home around these aspects. The individuality of your taste will then establish effortlessly a particular ambience – elegance perhaps, or prettiness. In time, as children grow up, or interests diversify, your environment will need to change too. We design our collections with an element of versatility so your decorative surroundings can evolve in keeping with a changing lifestyle.

Laura Ashley style is not about dictating a look to be slavishly imitated. It is rather about choosing a style that best suits the environment and brings out the character and essential charm of a room or house, as well as reflecting the lifestyle and individuality of the people living there. So whether you live in a rambling old house steeped in history or a modern architect-designed apartment, I hope that this book will be an enjoyable and inspiring guide to the endless possibilities of design and decoration.

Nick Ashley.

THE CREATION OF A STYLE

The name of Laura Ashley is recognized the world over for a design concept that is at once innovative and individual. Their Oxford Circus store, with its imposing facade, is at the very heart of the West End of London, one of the shopping capitals of Europe. Opened in 1985, it shows how the Laura Ashley philosophy permeates even shop design. Inside, seasoned mahogany is used for the fitments, and arrangements of flowers and music help to create a tranquil, almost country house environment in which to browse among the racks of clothes or view the inspirational roomsets – welcome refuge from the hustle and bustle of London's busiest shopping centre.

'Wild Clematis', like many of Laura Ashley's early positive-negative designs, took its inspiration from the minutiae of a bygone age – in this case, the endpaper pattern of a Victorian book.

Laura Ashley was a romantic, a sentimentalist, a traditionalist. Unashamed of her taste for nostalgia, she brought poetry and fantasy back into ordinary domestic life, liberating design from chrome, plastics and man-made fibres. 'For me the more faded and mellow the interior, the more beautiful it is,' she once wrote. 'I long for a newly decorated room to "settle down". Hand-made patchworks, needle-works, rag rugs, lace and white starched linens (together with old-fashioned smoothing irons) are all bliss to me. I have lived with slate floors for preference, strewn with gum boots, dogs and children, and at the same time managed to maintain the ritual of the dining room and the complete peace of comfortable bedrooms. These things turn a living environment into a home.'

Home: that was the magic word, the centre of Laura Ashley's values and philosophy. A Laura Ashley home might be simple and demure, or grandiose and daring; it might be furnished in humble cotton or the richest damask, but it should always be comfortable and welcoming. And it is appropriate that what is now a huge multi-national design and retailing business – one of Britain's great post-war success stories, in fact – should have started on the kitchen table of Laura and Sir Bernard Ashley's first, attic home in London's Pimlico, with an initial investment of £10.

The year was 1953: while Bernard Ashley went off to work in the City, his young wife Laura snatched time from looking after her children to produce tablemats and headscarves on a crude and laborious silk-screen machine, with the aim of selling them to local shops and department stores. And as the Ashley family grew – their four children are all connected in some capacity with the firm – so did business, albeit somewhat bumpily. A move into a nearby basement was accompanied by Bernard Ashley's development of more versatile dyeing and printing apparatus. Dress fabrics were now added to the repertoire. Bernard Ashley left his job to concentrate on running the financial side of matters and there was just enough money to employ Bert, a struggling painter, to help with the printing.

But for Laura Ashley a move back to her roots in the country became increasingly essential, and the family left London for an idyllic Surrey cottage set in an orchard and facing open farmlands. It was in this tranquil atmosphere, as she pored over eighteenth- and nineteenth-century print books, gathered swatches of material from old patchwork quilts, and copied motifs used to decorate ceramics and porcelain, that the Laura Ashley style began to germinate. Meanwhile, a factory was established in an old coach shed a few miles from the cottage, capable of housing larger machinery and stocks. Foreign customers began to show interest, and the enterprise prospered.

Then, in 1957, tragedy struck: a local river burst its banks and flooded the factory. Electric motors were destroyed, cloth was ruined, and the flood waters were dyed delicate shades of rose and lavender. It was a testing moment, but one which gave an opportunity for further change and development. For Laura Ashley, it was also a chance to return to her roots, her native hills of Wales. A choice had to be made between factory and house, so the Ashleys lived in a tent while saving the money to rent a rambling old house in Machynlleth, Montgomeryshire. Meanwhile, the factory was set up in nearby Carno.

The relationship between Laura Ashley and Wales proved a happy and lasting one. At first, there was some suspicion from the inhabitants of Carno. 'The Welsh have always been their own men,' Sir Bernard has recalled, 'and here they were staring over the fence at this weird English chap and his odd-looking machines in an old shed at Carno.' But they did not lean on that fence for long. Soon the Ashleys were employing a staff of ten and sales were topping £1,000 a week. Production and overhead costs were low, while quality control was high. Throughout the 1960s, the range of Laura Ashley products broadened and a certain 'look' became distinctly recognizable. Business continued to expand at a steady rate year by year.

In 1968, tired of retailers who would not or could not pay their bills, the Ashleys opened their first shop in Pelham Street, South Kensington; by 1986 there were over two hundred such establishments, from Paris to Tokyo, and from Sydney to San Francisco. That first acorn investment of £10 was now yielding a solid oak turnover of £100 million.

Yet if Laura Ashley was a big success, she continued to think small. A feeling for traditional craftsmanship has always marked her products – indeed, in the firm's early 'cottage industry' days, fabrics were printed and dyed on machines very similar to those in use a hundred or more years earlier. Laura Ashley's eye and taste were eclectic, always open to new influences, but they never led to a betrayal of those first principles of family and home.

Perhaps Laura Ashley's major source of inspiration was the cotton dress fabrics of the nineteenth century. In these she found a variety of trailing floral motifs, echoing the more expensive woven silks of the period, printed in one colour on a dotted or striped background. Such prints were used on the first Laura Ashley dresses, made in simple cotton, and they have continued to feature in subsequent Laura Ashley garment collections.

For the furnishing designs that followed, Laura Ashley began with deliberately naive 'rustic' prints, made from natural materials and printed in bold colours with traditional motifs. These have continued in the collections; but in 1983, with the introduction of a heavier weight of cotton fabric suitable for drawing rooms, Laura Ashley moved into the more formal areas of the house. Now, many of the new prints and colours were suitable not only for the bedrooms and bathrooms to

The Welsh countryside, with its rolling hills and verdant valleys, proved a profound influence on Laura Ashley's life and work, and remains to this day the key to the company's philosophy.

which most people had previously confined them, but also for the dining room and hall. For these new fabrics Laura Ashley developed prints with a rather more patrician ancestry than that of the earlier range. Prints such as 'Florentina', 'White Bower', 'Mr Jones' and 'Antoinette' had their origins in the *palazzi* of Florence, the printed silks of eighteenth-century Lyons and the pattern book of the Victorian designer and architect Owen Jones. They reflected a growing fascination with the past and an ever-deeper delving into country-house collections and museum archives.

Colour has also formed an important part of Laura Ashley style. From the very earliest days, Laura Ashley's aim was to create a *balanced* interior through the use of co-ordinating prints and colourways in fabrics and wallpapers. Those first simple designs, printed on strong colours, were often printed in reverse colours also, thus allowing the creation of a simple positive-and-negative monochrome scheme. As the collection expanded, the effect became one not of matching colours, but of colours designed to co-ordinate, providing an interior with a timeless quality, as though it had always looked that way. It is that same style of decoration known on the continent as *déshabillé anglaise* ('English undress'), and re-christened by interior decorator John Fowler as 'humble elegance'. It, too, represents an inspiration from the past, the revival of an element of English decoration that had been present as early as the 1670s.

Yet the Laura Ashley collection is not a historical showcase, however accurate and painstaking the research behind the designs and their reproduction might be. Mere antiquarian scholarship never interested Laura Ashley. With her designers she has been concerned, rather, to provide the means by which dreams can be turned into realities, bringing warmth, 'humble elegance' and charm into ordinary homes too long dominated by what author and critic Richard Hoggart called 'chain-store modernismus ... all bad veneer and sprayed-on varnish stain ... cold and ugly plastic door-handles; fussy and meaningless wall lampholders; metal tables which invite no-one and have their over-vivid colours kicked and scratched away: all tawdry and gimcrack.'

Against this chain-store ethic of the cheap and the disposable, Laura Ashley has taught a generation to appreciate the notion of prettiness. From her kitchen table in Pimlico she launched one of the most far-reaching revolutions in the history of modern design.

RUSTIC

STYLE

RUSTIC STYLE
Past Traditions

Throughout the Victorian era artists such as Myles Birket Foster and Henry Sylvester Stannard took delight in producing charming paintings which depict an English countryside of unprecedented prettiness and sentimental rusticity. This work by Stannard, entitled Sailing the Boat, *shows an idealized cottage exterior with its thatched roof, homely doves, a garden brimming over with cottage garden flowers such as hollyhocks and daisies, and a gently smoking chimney suggestive of warmth and comfort.*

The country cottage, roofed with thatch and covered with fragrant climbing roses, is an idealized image that has formed part of English decorative taste for the last two centuries. It is a style that exudes tranquillity, simplicity and permanence. Everything is made from natural materials – wood and stone, or burnished metals such as brass or pewter. The kitchen, with its open fireplace, is the heart of the home, and floral sprigs and gingham checks decorate walls and windows.

Over the past two decades, the appeal of the country cottage has grown significantly. But what of the traditional cottage interior, and the way in which it has developed over the centuries – rooms that have acquired their character and atmosphere from walls decorated with stencils, colourful hand-painted furniture and polished tile floors? The rustic tradition has been a spontaneous mixture of necessity, economy and the picturesque. The medieval labourer's cottage, the interiors of William Morris, the whimsical *cottages ornées* of Georgian England, the revival of the craft traditions of Europe and the America – all these elements have played a part in shaping a rustic style of interior decoration that spans both time and place, and can be re-created in the simplest of country cottages or the most modern city apartment □

The attraction of the simple life has always been strong whether it is that of Thoreau's backwoods in Massachusetts, complete with log cabin, or the play acting of the French aristocracy, done as always with great style. But it was in the sentimental climate of Victorian England that the idea of the rural idyll took strongest hold. Yet it bears very little relation to the way in which, throughout history, country folk have actually lived and furnished their dwellings.

Rustic Realities

The painting of scenes from English everyday life became popular from the early years of the nineteenth century. While the Victorian rendition of a rural lifestyle was far removed from reality, as can be seen in May Day *by S. Hayllar, elements of a true rustic style of decoration are still included: the cane-seated chairs, the tiled floor, the painted dresser with its ornamental plates and jugs, stoneware jars and simple candlestick. Even the beehives hint at country pursuits.*

In his Dictionary of 1755, Dr Johnson defined the cottage not as a charming rustic retreat, but as 'a hut or mean habitation'. What was the country cottage really like? Let us trace the story back to the beginning.

In Saxon times, most farm labourers simply ate and slept in the Great Hall of their master's house, and it was only after the Norman invasion that it became common for the villein or serf to build his own primitive cottage, a one-roomed windowless wooden structure, thatched with brush, heather or straw. In the fourteenth century, however, farm labourers began to experiment with a type of construction which followed in miniature that of the old Great Hall: stone foundations and timber frames supported thatched roofs and walls of dried mud,

plastered onto a framework of hazel or blackthorn, often known as 'wattle and daub'. Shutters of wickerwork or hide provided the only access to daylight.

The traditional early cottage plan consisted of one large room with sleeping quarters either above the living room, or adjacent to it. The centre of family life was the hearth, and the fire would be kept alight throughout the year. The best seat was that nearest to the fireplace and this privilege would only be surrendered to one's elders or guests. Food was cooked in a great pot suspended over the fire and bread would be baked in an oven set in the fireplace wall. Sanitation would have consisted only of an external 'earth privy'. Thatched roofs were almost universal, and this made an already fragile structure even more susceptible to fire. The actual living conditions remained bleak: the only furniture would have been a board on trestles for use as a table, and perhaps a few stools. The wood used was generally oak, which was durable and resistant to the harshness of the English climate.

This type of farm labourer's cottage was to form the basic habitation of the English rural community for the following five hundred years. There were some changes, however. In the sixteenth century, for instance, glass windows began to appear, but the tiny panes, fashioned from round flattened globules of molten glass, would not have admitted a great deal more light than the old wicker shutters. And from the late sixteenth century, dormers were often added to create an upper floor, frequently used not as a sleeping area, but as a workshop for small cottage industries which supplemented the limited agricultural income. It was also at this time that chimneys were added to cottages, thus reducing the risk of fire. But in general, any modifications of this kind provided improvements in interior comfort rather than outward appearance.

John Nash's Royal Lodge in Windsor Great Park, built in 1813 for the Prince Regent, represents the apotheosis of the early nineteenth-century vogue for the picturesque cottage ornée, *seen also in the work of Hope, Wyatville, Soane and Repton. Here, with the inclusion of superfluous Gothic detailing, numerous state rooms, roofs thatched for ornament rather than necessity, and perfectly kept lawns and flower gardens, Nash could hardly be more detached from the reality of the labourer's cottage without losing sight of his original inspiration.*

At its best, the cottage might have been furnished with wooden shelves displaying a warming pan, tankards, pewter or wooden plates, iron pots, and a couple of candlesticks. The only decoration would have been a few scraps of a floral-printed lining paper hung on the walls, a distant forerunner of wallpaper as we know it today.

At its everyday worst, however, families of a dozen or more would have huddled together in a miserable hut of clay and straw with a leaking roof and a draughty, wooden-slatted door, prey to cold, hunger and disease.

The Rustic Idyll

It was in the eighteenth century that the landowning classes first developed a taste for the rustic idyll, romanticizing the cottage and the 'joys' of rustic life. In literature the fashion was not a new one – the Garden of Eden was the original pastoral setting, and Classical writers such as Theocritus and Virgil, much imitated in the Renaissance, presented charming pictures of shepherds leading lives of innocent and perpetual peace and happiness. The contrast of court and country life is a theme of Shakespeare's *As You Like It* and *The Winter's Tale*, and runs through seventeenth- and eighteenth-century poetry.

One of the earliest examples of the early nineteenth-century cottage ornée was the rustic dairy at Hamels Park, Hertfordshire, an English parallel to the petit hameau of Marie Antoinette. Constructed by Sir John Soane in 1781, it is now sadly lost. Unmistakeably Neo-classical in conception, its thatched roof, rounded end bays and iron-transomed windows serve to connect it to a rustic heritage.

There was a general move among the cultured away from the gilded extravagance of the Baroque towards an appreciation of the natural. Inspired by the Arcadian vision of artists such as Salvator Rosa and Claude Lorraine, landowners like Henry Hoare of Stourhead in Wiltshire combined winding paths and artificial lakes with temples, urns and statuary to re-create the golden age. For the eighteenth-century landscape gardener 'Capability' Brown, beauty lay in the undulating lines of nature, which he re-created in his own idealized landscapes by means of sweeping greenswards, vast lakes and carefully grouped trees. It may have looked natural: it was of course highly artificial – and expensive – as were the rustic cottages that began to appear, along with the grottos and follies of the Picturesque movement, and which were, more often than not, never intended for human habitation. What mattered about the delightful Gothic cottage of Alfred's Hall at Cirencester, for example, created by the poet Alexander Pope in 1721, was its look of quaintness and antiquity, not its practicality as a building in which to live.

This form of indulgent garden folly was carried even further in the *petit hameau* which Marie Antoinette had built in the grounds of Versailles, a 'rustic village' complete with thatched cottages and a little mill. The interiors of this little hamlet were papered with small floral designs of pinks, violets and other wild flowers. All were carefully weathered with

This early Victorian genre painting by Frederick Daniel Hardy, The Foreign Guest, *is unusual in its relatively realistic treatment of the subject of the interior of a country labourer's cottage, and includes a great deal of interesting detail. The central focus of attention is the large, simple fireplace, with its plain cloth hanging and single shelf on which are displayed an assortment of treasures and household items. Before the fire stands a rush-seated chair beside a simple oak table, covered with a plain white tablecloth. The windows are uncovered, but wrapped around the baby's cradle is a colourful patchwork quilt. The 'foreign guest' brings with him a painted chest of drawers, an example of another rustic tradition.*

painted cracks to complete the illusion. It was here that she delighted in playing the shepherdess (carrying a gold-tipped crook) or milkmaid (carrying a solid silver bucket) at a convenient distance from her magnificent state apartments in the palace itself.

But it was in the early nineteenth century that the cult of the picturesque reached its apotheosis with the *cottage ornée*. The most famous example of this vogue for a rustic life style was undoubtedly that designed in 1813 by John Nash for the Prince Regent in Windsor Great Park, known today as the Royal Lodge. But it was an architectural style which spread further than the aristocratic echelons of society. When a character in Jane Austen's *Sense and Sensibility* declares 'I am excessively fond of a cottage; there is always so much comfort, so much elegance about them,' he is thinking not of the real 'mean habitations' of farm labourers, but the contemporary decorative cottages that sprang up on the outskirts of cities as well as in the country. Asymmetrical, and studded with 'Gothic' detailing and lead casement windows, such cottages were high Regency chic. They might have been as small as a genuine cottage or as large as a medium-sized house with as many as fifteen rooms. Endsleigh in Devon, built in 1810 by Sir Jeffry Wyatville, is a perfect example of the type and clearly a pure fantasy for the sophisticated middle class.

This country style was soon affected in dress and decoration as well, and it became fashionable practice for a gentleman to wear a country riding coat in town, regardless of his equestrian proficiency, while portrait painters were called upon to depict their subjects seated on 'rustic' chairs which retained their faded gingham check covers.

Meanwhile, in continental Europe a similar taste for simplicity was to be seen, though it had somewhat different underlying causes. Following the defeat of Napoleon in 1815, the chaos that was the aftermath of twenty years of war made simplicity of decoration an economic necessity for many of the impoverished families of Europe. In Austria and Germany the resultant style has been labelled Biedermeier – after a fictitious newspaper columnist and arbiter of taste – and it is characterized by its functional, geometric yet elegant appearance and its restraint of ornament. It was a style that reached across society, blurring the distinctions between prosperity and poverty.

Ironically, all this simulated rusticity came at a time when the authentic peasant skills of cottage building were in decline. Instead private programmes of estate redevelopment provided new housing for tenants and labourers. However, the motives behind the construction of these 'model villages' were not entirely philanthropic.

In the first half of the eighteenth century the most common reason for the construction of new rural housing had been the owners' desire to remove the unsightly and disorderly variety of tenants' cottages, scattered over their carefully 'improved' landscaped parks. An early example was set by Lord Orford at Chippenham in 1702, and in 1724 Sir Robert Walpole built New Houghton with two-storied workers' cottages of red brick. In 1773 Sir William Chambers designed Milton Abbas in Dorset, which was later modified with the addition of thatched roofs by 'Capability' Brown. Even the great country house architect Robert Adam was involved in the construction of such new 'model' villages: Lowther, in Cumbria, was built by him in 1770. In 1794 Sir Uvedale Price exhorted landlords to erect more model villages as 'sources of amusement and interest', and it was as such that they were primarily regarded – charming additions to the landscape, built in the same spirit of academic fancy as that which had inspired a previous generation to fill their parks with classical temples and follies.

A few building schemes did have a more serious economic purpose: one example is to be found at Harewood in West Yorkshire, where the three-storied houses and cottages were designed to incorporate workrooms for ribbon-makers. During the early nineteenth century many cottage pattern books were published to aid prospective builder/landlords. But sympathetic concern for the filthy conditions in which most cottagers lived was only secondary. The interiors of these model cottages differed little from the original dwellings they replaced. At Milton Abbas each cottage accommodated an average of four families, with the result that as many as forty people might share one four-roomed cottage. The front door would have opened straight into a sitting room, used only 'for best'. Here there might be a dresser with a few dishes, a mantelpiece lined with crude pottery ornaments, and on the floor a simple rag rug. The walls would have been hung with framed proverbs and quotations from the Bible, sometimes picked out in needlework. At the back of the cottage was the everyday living room with a huge cast iron range and a stone sink. It was only in the middle of the nineteenth century that attention to the well-being of the inhabitants allowed a happier balance to be struck between picturesque exteriors and interior comfort and convenience. At Old Warden in Bedfordshire, built in the 1850s, for instance, the cottages are not only carefully integrated into the surrounding landscape, but are also spacious and light with sound thatches.

Throughout the nineteenth century, the realization that the look of old England – 'Merry England' – had been destroyed by the mills and factories spawned by the Industrial Revolution, by the transformation of ancient common ground into more productive arable land, as well as by the activities of 'improving' landscapers, led to an increased pressure to conserve the remnants of a lost past. 'We have a tendency to mourn the disappearance of places we have never seen, or of which we know nothing,' wrote the art historian John Pope-Hennessy, and a weakness of Victorian culture was its inclination to bathe the Middle Ages in particular in a golden haze of chivalry, sentiment and romance. The Merry England of rose-covered cottages on the village green that

The walls of the country cottage would have been hung with few images. However, among these one would almost certainly have found a sampler. This rather poignant piece of work executed as the first, and presumably the last effort at needlework of a young country girl, destined like so many of her kind to die tragically young, unites in its imagery the rural preoccupations of church and countryside. Around two typically nineteenth-century religious texts are depicted birds, butterflies, flowers and trees in a variety of natural colours.

romantics tried to preserve or re-create had never actually existed – but did that matter? The effect that such dreams and fictions had on visual taste and domestic interiors was richly productive.

Two of the most important names in the first stages of this movement were the Welsh architect Owen Jones (1809–74), and the philanthropist Henry Cole (1808–82), both committed to what the great architect and philosopher of Victorian Gothic A.W.N.Pugin had called 'true principles' of design. Cole crowned his career by becoming the first director of the Victoria and Albert Museum in South Kensington, the world's first museum of the applied and decorative arts and an institution inspired by the success of the Great Exhibition of 1851. Previously in 1847 he had established Summerly's Art Manufactures, an enterprise in which he collaborated with several like-minded artists to 'revive the good old practice of connecting the best art with familiar objects in daily use . . . to decorate each article with appropriate details . . . and to obtain these details as directly as possible from nature'. Jones, who achieved widespread influence through his book *The Grammar of Ornament*, published in 1856, stressed the values of truth to materials and high standards of craftsmanship. The further conclusion of both Cole and Jones on the matter of 'true principles' was that it was perfectly possible to decorate an entire interior using features selected from a number of disparate sources, as indeed country people had been doing in their own cottages for several centuries. The activities and ideas of Pugin, Cole, Jones and the artists associated with Summerly's, alongside the showcase of the Great Exhibition, resulted in a growing appreciation of the virtues of the English vernacular style among the upper and middle classes; and it was in the 1860s, with the emergence of the writings of a younger man, that all the elements of the rustic style finally crystallized into a coherent design philosophy that was to have a decisive and lasting effect upon popular taste in interior decoration. That man was William Morris.

One of the most influential areas of William Morris's work was the design of fabrics and wallpapers. 'Jasmine Trellis', with its pattern of carefully delineated jasmine flowers intertwining around a wicker trellis, provides a good example of the type of popular design that would have appealed to the urban middle classes of the latter half of the nineteenth century.

William Morris

Cole and Jones had both tried to establish a place for machine-made, mass-produced materials and objects in the future of design: this was the point at which Morris parted company with them. His express aim was to restore traditional crafts and methods to a society in which he saw modern mechanical industry destroying 'man's natural purpose and sense of life'.

As a young man, Morris (1834–96) was prominent in the circle that gathered around the Pre-Raphaelite Brotherhood, a group of English artists including Holman Hunt, John Millais, the Rossettis, and later Edward Burne-Jones who, in the 1850s, declared their intention 'to

In 1861, William Morris established the firm of Morris, Marshall, Faulkner & Co. to produce furniture and objects which would embody the English country furnishing tradition. Together with the architect Philip Webb, Morris created furniture types which were to exert a profound and far-reaching influence upon English, European and American design. This watercolour of Burne-Jones's London dining room, painted by his studio assistant T. M. Rooke, shows the unmistakeable characteristics of the Arts and Crafts style. The principle wood used was oak, not inlaid but plain, or boldly painted with traditional rural motifs or scenes from British folklore. Set against floral wallpapers, furniture forms were simply turned and splayed, and the unupholstered chairs had traditional rush seats. Burne-Jones himself painted the sideboard as well as designing the stained glass windows, while the dining-room table was designed by Philip Webb.

study Nature attentively so as to know how to express *genuine* ideas'. In this they were both inspired and supported by the art critic John Ruskin, whose thoughts had a profound influence on Victorian attitudes. Like Morris, Ruskin deplored the effects of industrialization and all decorative 'falsehoods'. 'Go to nature in all singleness of heart, selecting nothing, rejecting nothing,' he preached in his *Modern Painters* (1846). Closely linked to this was the idea that all work should be 'well finished' and charged with moral significance. The Pre-Raphaelite Brotherhood expressed this philosophy in their paintings in which the people of the countryside are shown in idealized surroundings.

In 1861, having been associated with the Pre-Raphaelites for five years, Morris decided that their ideals, and those of Ruskin, should be taken further. He founded the firm of Morris, Marshall, Faulkner & Co., producing furniture, textiles, glassware, ceramics and metalwork in a firmly English vernacular style, incorporating motifs of birds, flowers, fruit and foliage. His designs received wide acclaim, but Morris, a pioneering socialist, was already worried by the fact that it was mainly the rich who seemed to be taking them up and using them in their interiors. 'What business have we with art at all unless we can share it?' he asked. The search for an answer to that question coloured the rest of his life's work.

Morris's own house in Bexleyheath makes an interesting commentary on his thoughts about interior decoration. The Red House, as it is still known, was designed by his architect friend Philip Webb in 1859. In its day it was revolutionary. Its manner is notably simple and unrelieved, more like a farmhouse than the customary gentleman's residence in classical or Gothic taste. Webb and Morris aimed for comfort rather than elegance and a feeling of the rough and spontaneous which one finds in native rustic building. Morris clothed this framework with his own lucid and uncomplicated fabrics and papers, in militant reaction against the stuffy academicism of the mainstream of mid-Victorian style. Materials were of local origin wherever possible, and plain and humble with it. Pewter and brass were the favoured metals; English woods such as oak and beech, combined with cane and rush, were used for the chairs; traditional English simplicity characterized the furniture – trestle tables, wooden settles and Welsh dressers. Towards the end of his life Morris wrote: 'I have tried to produce goods which should be genuine ... woollen substances as woollen as possible, cotton as cottony as possible ... I have used only the dyes which are natural and simple, because they produce beauty almost without the intervention of art.'

Morris devoted himself to spreading this gospel. All about him he saw poverty, slum housing, overcrowding and appalling working conditions, the ruination of the countryside and the birth of a new society whose products were shoddy, cheap and temporary. 'Men living amidst such ugliness,' he declared, 'cannot conceive of beauty,' and until his death in 1896 he strove to realize his dream of a land in which 'simplicity of life' would beget 'simplicity of taste'. 'Having nothing in your house which is not beautiful' was the ethic he preached. Morris died a frustrated man, but his dream has lived on.

Arts and Crafts

Morris's influence was an important factor in the development of what is now remembered as the Arts and Crafts movement, although it was Ruskin's formation in 1872 of the Guild of St George, a sort of non-

Walter Crane's frontispiece to The House Beautiful, *which first appeared in America in 1896. This edition also included articles and designs by Morris, Voysey and Ashbee, and helped to publicize the Arts and Crafts movement in America, where Crane's work was greatly admired. An associate of Morris, and member of the Art Workers' Guild, Crane was also a designer of wallpapers, fabrics, tapestries, carpets and ceramic tiles as well as a celebrated book illustrator.*

political trades union of furniture-makers and decorative craftsmen, that set the trend. This was followed in 1882 by the Century Guild, led by A. H. Mackmurdo and Selwyn Image, which made a special feature of natural forms, chiefly floral, on fabrics; then in 1884 came the Art Workers' Guild, set up by the architect Richard Norman Shaw, the designer William Lethaby, and the artist Walter Crane. Its aims were 'to advance education in all the visual arts and crafts . . . and to foster and maintain high standards of design and craftsmanship'. Finally, in 1888, the Combined Arts Committee was formed. This became the Arts and Crafts Society, which numbered among its members C. R. Ashbee, Walter Crane and Ernest Gimson.

Their chosen period of inspiration was the Middle Ages, at which time – or so they fondly believed – artistic creativity had been part of everyone's daily life, with every humble cottage full of cherished and useful artefacts, made not bought: in other words, the polar opposite of the mass-produced knick-knackery that sat on every suburban Victorian mantelpiece.

The Arts and Crafts movement gradually shifted its focus away from the fog and smoke of the metropolis and gravitated towards the quaint rural villages of the Cotswolds. Ashbee settled in the golden-stoned village of Chipping Campden with a team of craftsmen from London's East End. Specializing in metalwork and jewellery, Ashbee produced designs based on an imaginary world with traits of the eighteenth-century Picturesque style. But these were not *objets d'art* for connoisseurs – at least, not in theory: behind everything the Arts and Crafts disciples made and thought was the hope that the tastes and lives of the poorer classes could be enriched by access to the 'useful and right, pleasantly shaped and finished, good enough, but not too good for everyday use'.

The movement ranged wide over all areas of the fine and decorative arts: Walter Crane was another of Morris's pupils, whose illustrations for children's books served to popularize the rural revival, and whose flower and plant designs ornamented the ceramics of William de Morgan, Wedgwood and Minton.

Charles Annesley Voysey was another important figure. He had originally trained as an architect in the academic Gothic style, but the teachings of Morris dramatically changed his outlook. In 1882 he set himself up as a designer, concentrating on textiles and wallpapers and creating such designs as 'Bird and Tulip' and 'Let us Prey', using the by-now customary bird and plant forms. But his most clearly identifiable and individual work came in the field of furniture. His simple pieces, with their use of unstained oak, clean, tapered uprights surmounted by an angular platform, and flowing convex horizontals possess a rare austerity and grace. Ernest Gimson's celebrated rush-seated chair of 1896, a landmark in furniture design, shows Voysey's influence.

Charles Annesley Voysey's designs for fabrics and wallpapers reveal the profound influence of William Morris in their unrestrained use of birds and foliage. In such examples as this design for a printed linen of about 1893, Voysey displays a supreme stylization that is not generally present in the majority of Morris's own designs.

RIGHT *and* BELOW *While this Viennese drawing room of the 1840s, with its floral wallpaper and simple cotton curtains, echoes an earlier eighteenth-century obsession with the rural idyll, Carl Larsson's watercolour of a Swedish interior reflects a very different folk heritage.*

The Arts and Crafts movement was not confined to England. In Scandinavia, a similar response had been taking place. As early as 1845 an enlightened Swedish government had foreseen the likely effects of industrialization on a strong tradition, and had taken steps to preserve it. A Swedish Society of Arts and Crafts was formed for the close collaboration of art and industry and for the general raising of Swedish national cultural awareness. Around the turn of the century the painter Carl Larsson published *The House in the Sun*, a collection of watercolours depicting the interiors of his country cottage in the heart of rural Sweden, which were decorated in a light and simple style using traditional Swedish craftsmanship and materials. His watercolours were enormously popular throughout Europe.

In Germany another influential book of interiors was *The English House* by Herman Muthesius, published in 1904. It acquainted the general public of Germany with the English Arts and Crafts style, in particular the bold rustic designs of Philip Webb, architect of Morris's Red House. This book, together with the work of several British designers then active in Germany, including M. H. Baillie Scott, MacLachlan and J. A. Campbell, had a great effect on German interiors in the early 1900s and the English vernacular style was taken up and imaginatively reinterpreted by young German designers such as Paul Stosseck.

In the United States, several movements arose that took their primary inspiration from the Arts and Crafts idea, two of the most significant being Gustav Stickley's 'Craftsman' style and Elbert Hubbard's 'Roycrofter' movement. In New York Stickley publicized the look

BELOW *Painting and stencilling are an important part of the American rustic furnishing tradition. Early settlers used stencilled decoration on floors and walls to decorate their simple clapboard houses. Furniture was also decorated in this way, motifs being taken from the surrounding countryside.*

BELOW *In 1901, Gustav Stickley launched* The Craftsman, *a periodical designed to popularize the Arts and Crafts style of decoration. A craft traditional to nineteenth-century rural America was quilt-making, which became quite a social occasion amongst farming communities, especially when it involved a bridal quilt like the colourful Baltimore example below. Executed in cotton and using a shaded blue fabric called Rainbow or Fondu cloth, each square would have been sewn by a different hand.*

through a monthly periodical, *The Craftsman*, in which watercolours showed the simple countrified appearance of various Arts and Crafts rooms in the 'English Cottage' manner. Although their work was short-lived – *The Craftsman* closed in 1916 and Hubbard had drowned on the *Lusitania* the previous year – they did open American eyes to a forgotten rural heritage.

'Rustic Charm' in the Suburbs

Outside the Arts and Crafts movement, its homespun nature and socialistic aspirations, more mainstream craftsmen, artists and architects also felt the pull of the vernacular and the rustic. For example, out of the *cottage ornée* style of the Regency period grew 'Old English' style, whose major exponent was the architect Norman Shaw. In 1868 he designed a house at Leys Wood in Sussex which combined elements of fifteenth-, sixteenth-, and seventeenth-century architecture in a *tour de force* of 'old Englishness'. The rooms were deliberately set at irregular heights and the dining room contained a huge inglenook fireplace. Outside one finds adaptations of such traditional features as half-timbering, hung tiles and hipped roofs, as well as pargetting – the technique of plastering gable ends with incised lines or embossed patterns, commonly seen on authentic Essex cottages. On the inside a vogue for faded and tattered fabrics and 'distressed' furniture continued the country tradition.

One of the most complete examples of Old English style was Bedford Park in Chiswick, West London. Here Shaw, along with his colleague Jonathan Carr, built what has been called 'the first garden suburb' – an entire estate composed of English vernacular styles and decorated with designs by Morris & Co. A deliberate lack of symmetry gives each house on the estate its own individual character, in imitation of the 'improvised' look of country cottages. Similar developments soon became a standard feature throughout the middle-class areas of English city suburbs. So although Morris and his followers may never have succeeded in redeeming the poorer members of society, they certainly improved the middle-class eye. Ashbee found few buyers for arts and crafts in the villages of the Cotswolds or the slums of the East End; but he did establish a profitable relationship with the furniture designer Sir Ambrose Heal who, in the early 1900s, began to show Ashbee's designs in the family shop in Tottenham Court Road, London, thus giving Arts and Crafts products the advertising they needed. Heal was impressed by Ashbee's integrity, his high standards and respect for raw materials and native woods. When he became chairman of his family company in 1913, he insisted that Ashbee's principles remain paramount in the selection of designs for sale.

Although a few purists made attempts to preserve a truly vernacular style as the century progressed, it came to look increasingly ridiculous. Many artists of the younger generation, who had been brought up in the shadow of Morris and Ashbee, moved on to become exponents of the more stylized form of decoration known as Art Nouveau, described by the old-school rustic Walter Crane as a 'strange decadent disease' and yet one which filled so many Edwardian houses with rural motifs, sinuously re-interpreted and elaborated.

BELOW The Studio's Year Book of Decorative Art, *published in 1919, was devoted to cottage design and decoration. Simplicity and comfort were the key elements: simple woven curtains, patchwork bedcovers and wooden furniture were advocated for these cottage schemes, with colourful additions of pictures, pottery and fabrics. The choice of pottery and china was dictated by well-designed shapes and single, glazed colours, such as those seen in designs from the Ravenscourt Pottery.*

Rustic Revival

It was not, however, the decadence of Art Nouveau that was the final nail in the coffin of the rustic style, but the First World War. After 1918, the world was clearly a different place in which to live. With the emancipation of women, a dearth of domestic servants, the arrival of the motor car and other technological developments, the image of home as a cosy family refuge was radically altered. Interior decoration in the 1920s and 1930s became steadily more attuned to the modern age. One trend succeeded another with ever-increasing speed: revivals, adaptations and imports, both inventive and derivative. Change was all, and the stability represented by the old farm labourer's cottage now seemed evidence only of poverty and primitivism.

The one strand of rustic revivalism that did continue to flourish stemmed from Carr and Shaw's Bedford Park, and the idea of the garden suburb. Throughout the 1930s, in developments like Petts Wood in Kent, plots were filled with houses whose exteriors boasted the country cottage conventions of weather-boarding, 'timber' and leaded windows, while inside they contained mass-produced reproductions of hand-turned oak furniture and exposed beams, brick fireplaces in which gas-powered log fires would flame merrily, and a glorious hotch-potch of Victorian chintz, fake Jacobean furniture and 'Regency' French windows! It was this mock Tudor revival that Osbert Lancaster labelled 'By-pass Variegated' in his satirical history of architecture, *Pillar to Post.*

The tranquil image of the idyllic, rose-covered cottage was again shattered by a second world war. The consequent necessity of rehousing enormous numbers of people, in a very short period of time, and at the least possible expense, meant that any style except the functional was unattainable for the majority of Europeans in the 1940s and 1950s.

It was not until the 1960s, with a general relaxation of tension at all levels of culture and society, that a reaction against the 'soullessness' of the 'machine age' set in. An ever-increasing fascination with the past, as

This typical rustic interior is not in fact taken from an actual cottage but a scheme for the design of a kitchen proposed by Waring and Gillow in the 1920s. One would be forgiven for mistaking this for the genuine article, for here are all the traditional elements of rustic style in a twentieth-century context: the inviting hearth with its black-leaded stove and high mantelshelf; the dresser crammed with simple stoneware pottery; the unfussy, turned-wood Windsor chairs and a sturdy table covered with a linen tablecloth. Plain walls are hung with an array of brass pots, and simple cotton curtains grace the window. The wooden furnishings are painted in a subtle shade of green, further emphasizing the rustic character of a kitchen which would be equally at home in a smart city apartment or in the heart of the country.

seen in Victorian, Edwardian, Art Nouveau and Art Deco revivals, led to a renewal of interest in past methods of design. The escapism of the rural idyll became the spirit of the day: many young people left the city for the country and a simpler, communal way of life; small craft workshops were set up, and folk art and music thrived, and in 1975 Peter Blake, the erstwhile Pop artist, founded the Brotherhood of the Ruralists in the West Country.

A great vogue for the Victorian countryside reached into all aspects of everyday life from clothes to decorating to the packaging of products. Furniture styles echoed the bentwood and stripped pine of the 1900s. Walls were either colour-washed or papered in a light floral print. This taste for the rustic in the 1970s was pioneered by Laura Ashley, and it was a style that came to be epitomized by the traditional Laura Ashley look of simple, stylized floral sprigs with a muted colour palette of mid-tone, earthy colours such as smoke and plum. Her designs were produced in the same spirit as that of the Arts and Crafts movement, with an attention to finish and an insistence on natural materials. The very names of the prints themselves – 'Wild Cherry', 'Meadow Flowers', 'Oak Leaves' – are all full of the freshness and colour of the countryside.

Laura Ashley brought the country back to the city, allowing every home to recapture at least a visual reminder of a rustic dream that may never have existed in reality, but which will continue to provide an enchanting escape from the imperfections of the present.

RUSTIC STYLE
Laura Ashley

Samplers provide a valuable record of changing fashions in needlework, but they are equally important as a visual diary of contemporary events and family life. Rustic motifs such as flowers, animals, trees and birds, often within a floral border, were frequently used in Victorian samplers, as were sayings and proverbs. This example, probably c. 1840 and most likely made by a child, hangs from a length of cotton fabric, tied in a simple bow – perfectly appropriate for an attic bedroom.

The traditions of simple English country life formed the inspiration for the very first Laura Ashley designs, those small floral prints which became known and loved the world over, and whose naive simplicity greatly influenced the interiors of the 1970s.

As a decorative tradition, rustic style has always been characterized by its use of the colours of the countryside, the lovingly handcrafted – whether it be woven textiles, polished beams, limed floorboards or simple rush-seated chairs. It is a tradition where even the most humble household object takes on an intrinsic importance, blending the decorative and the functional.

For Laura Ashley, rustic style is unpretentious, welcoming and comfortable, an informal style that is conveyed with a colourful mixture of prints and textures. The scullery of a Welsh farmhouse owes its clean freshness to the classic simplicity of black and white stripes and cherry patterns; a Long Island bedroom has a rustic, hand-printed look, its designs taken from trunk linings and quilt patterns; tones of warm terracotta and dark green reflect the earthy colours of the American rustic tradition, while a wooden chalet in the heart of the Swiss countryside contains all the colour of Alpine scenery in its bright blue, crimson and green colour scheme □

A country attic bedroom encapsulates all the charms of the rustic way of life. Natural light streams in from a simple dormer window, highlighting the well-polished steel bedstead, with its late nineteenth-century quilt. Dark oak floorboards are covered with a simple North Country rag rug, and the whole effect is brightened by the prettiness of lightly-flowered wallpaper and fabrics in muted shades of smoke blue and cream. A crisply starched, white lace cloth covers the small table and a simple earthenware jug of freshly-gathered meadow flowers completes the scene.

Though this is the kitchen of a French chateau, it is delightfully unimposing and robust in nature. Light streams in from a lofty window and everything is on a generous scale. The chief decorative feature of the room is the old-fashioned sideboard, above which is displayed a host of familiar treasures: plates are propped up behind enamel coffee pots, blue-tinged glass bottles, Toby jugs, glazed earthenware, copper pie dishes, brown Dutch tiles and even an old flat iron. It is the kitchen equivalent of a cabinet of curiosities. On the table is a similar disarray of the prosaic, the edible and the elegant. A real love of nature is all-pervasive with the fringe of dried flowers simply pinned above and the strings of garlic which frame the whole. The light-coloured wood gives the room a contemporary feel. But it is the big beech table, heaped with glorious produce, that captures the eye in this moss green kitchen.

A rustic bathroom such as this can be as much at home in a large country house as in a small country cottage. And rustic style need not be confined to sprigs. The bathroom is an ideal room for choosing the seaside equivalent of a flower-sprigged meadow – a shell-scattered beach. Naive blue and white tiles take a pattern of tip-tilted shells up to a blue painted shelf, and matching wallpaper carries it above to the ceiling. The same motif is picked up on the Victorian bath, its stencilled shells dancing above a 'sea' of sapphire paint.

A soft note is introduced with a leaf-printed cotton, which is used as a fabric skirt for the wash basin and as a frilled festoon blind, its curved swags echoing the garland pattern on the cornice. The battered laundry basket gives the room character, while a great sheaf of corn in a driftwood basket together with a heap of real shells evoke potent memories of nature and the sea. China plates in a bathroom may seem curious, but not only are their simple patterns entirely right for this rustic bathroom, their fine, glazed texture plays up the similar surfaces of bath, wash basin and tiles. Finally, the scrubbed and bleached floorboards give an air of salt-sea cleanliness.

A room fit for the pleasant but serious business of eating. Venerable English oak dominates and darkens the scene to give a due sense of dignity. This is brightened by the prettiness of lightly-flowered wallpaper and fabrics in quiet shades of jade, sand and soft crimson. The heavy chairs are smartly dressed with frilled and fitted tie-on seat covers and chairback cushions. They stand on a stone floor, whose rock-like texture and colour emphasize the use of natural materials in this dining room, and reflect the pure quality of a northern light. The darkly glowing colours of the pewter and ironwork add to the subdued mood. On the solid oak mantelshelf stands an ironwork candlestick, pewter coffee pots and other drinking vessels. The simplicity of the black chandelier, made from reclaimed tin, gives a countrified feel to what is usually a rather grand object. There is no electricity and the lovely touch of real candles underlines the genuine nature of the room.

By the window stands a traditional dresser stacked with plates that pinpoint the crimson and jade shades of the overall colour scheme. The window seat is an informal corner, a resting place for that essential rustic accessory – a dog.

This young girl's bedroom is imbued with all the nostalgia and dreaminess associated with the transition from childhood to adulthood. Whimsical remembrances of the nursery, such as the doll's house, are mingled with something as grown-up and exciting as a real four-poster bed complete with canopy and curtains. Yet there is a natural progression from the imaginative games of childhood to the romantic thrill of sleeping in such a fairytale bower.

A stencilled frieze of rambling roses unifies the room, conveying both femininity and a rustic innocence of form. This is balanced by a *faux* braid border beneath the picture rail. A blithe rose-and-trellis pattern has been chosen for the wallpaper and fabric to give overall youthfulness, and the diamond shape of the trellis is repeated on the stencilled floor.

An abundance of demure frills is added by the flounces of a festoon blind. The bed hangings are restful – subdued plum and cream rather than the traditional pink – and pick up the overall colour scheme. A painted chest of drawers makes a pretty change from polished wood, and the 1840 Boston rocker is an amusing counterpoint to the antique rocking-horse. An evocative room.

This American parlour incorporates all the love of simplicity and nature-inspired pattern characteristic of rustic interiors. Yet in many ways the style of this Long Island house owes much to the American Federal period. It was a nineteenth-century quilt which inspired the printed cotton used on sofa, curtains and cushions, while the paper border of formal leaves is also true to the Federal type. The parlour has all the mellowness of autumnal colours: primrose and apricot stippled wallpaper, a salmon-coloured chair and cinnamon cushion. The bare boards and limed fireplace reflect the early American ascetic taste while the rug thrown over the sofa creates a casual air.

The parlour adjoins a complementary dining room where a sprightly, stylized tulip print on walls and blind gives a cool freshness to the room. Real fruit and flowers bring the room to life and a print framed in pale grey wood enhances the rustic tone.

This is country living in the Swiss vernacular in an unspoilt fifteenth-century chalet. What stamps it as Swiss is the marvellous wooden cosiness – like being inside a spice box. The warmth of simple panelling is enhanced by the colourful printed cottons used to decorate the room. Rich crimson and deep mustard are the key colours with a light note of sapphire blue. Colours that are subordinate in one design are taken as the main hue in another to create a unified rhythm. Armchairs and sofa are covered in a subtly mottled crimson; cushions are covered in red berries or flowers with sapphire leaves, and the sapphire stripe is picked up in the settle seat cover.

The same ad hoc principle is applied to the furniture. Rustic style is not a formal one; it is the happy union of disparate elements which gives it its special charm. Thus the settle, marriage chest and splay-legged table are rough-hewn country pieces, whereas sofa and armchairs are in an altogether more polished idiom. The marriage chest, inscribed with hearts and the names 'Hanset Luciriede' and 'Ursina Polcasper', displays a collection of china portraying the pastoral idyll.

This Welsh farmhouse scullery is the homeliest room in the house. It is a country workroom where jobs such as washing, scrubbing, dressing game and making butter and cheese are done. Watering-cans are stored here together with neat stacks of clay pots and a tub of pegs; a poacher's basket hangs by its stout leather strap, and more baskets are suspended from the beams ready to be swept down for laundry duty on the drying-green.

The deep china sink standing on plain white bricks holds armfuls of freshly-cut flowers. Next to it, a pestle and mortar, sitting in an old-fashioned wooden butter churn, catches the whey from curd cheese, hung up in muslin from a butcher's hook.

The no-nonsense, workaday look is achieved by the freshness of black and white. The cherry sprig wallpaper, based on a nineteenth-century dress print, is cheerful but crisp. A liquorice-striped ticking is used for curtains, seat covers and fabric skirt. (Country people often used to hang a cotton skirt where they could not afford cupboards.) Old, fissured and worn, the quarry-tiled floor leads up to the stairs where the house proper begins.

This master bedroom in Long Island, New York, epitomizes the strong, individual character of American rustic style. The traditional colours of the early American nation, blue and light stone, were used throughout the Federal period on everything from waistcoat linings to furniture. The simple curtains, with their looped headings hang from a pine pole. Their dot and square print, originally used on popular tablecloths, has also been used for the bedhangings with a smart co-ordinating border. A symmetrical dot design, discovered on the lining of a trunk, has been used for the valance, armchair and drape linings. The cushions are covered in a traditional gingham country check and a delicate botanical print, both in the same co-ordinating tones of blue and stone.

All the designs have a rustic, hand-printed appearance, firmly expressive of the tradition that fills this historic old house, with its Shaker-style rushlights, simple fire surround and wide pine boards.

The small bedroom leading off the master bedroom has all the appearance of a nineteenth-century sea captain's cabin. Curtains, wall and bed are all covered in a neat three-colour stripe, while the armchair is covered in a lively print of small diamonds and leaves on a terracotta ground. A touch of variety is added by the bolster on the wooden bed.

The rustic idiom stretches from country cottage to the rather more measured style of a gentleman farmer's residence. This is the point where the freshness and quaintness of the country meets the assurance and decorativeness of the country house, a style that falls somewhere between dimity prints with whitewashed wainscots and rococo swags with panelled walls. The hall of this Provençal farmhouse is in such a style, where formal elements are arranged casually against a mellow background.

A rustic mood is evoked in the unpainted, natural surfaces of the wooden shutters, the twisted, carved column and the soft worn greys and fawns of the stone-flagged floor. Walls, curtains and tablecloth are all in the same print, scattered with pretty flowers associated with country style, and the linking arabesques of delicate leaves and stems which have a more sophisticated provenance. The colour combination is elegant and sober – spice brown with gentle reds and blues. Burgundy gimp edges everything to unify the room. On the table, an unglazed terracotta urn holds not formal garden flowers but hedgerow clippings, and fruit is arranged in simple wooden bowls.

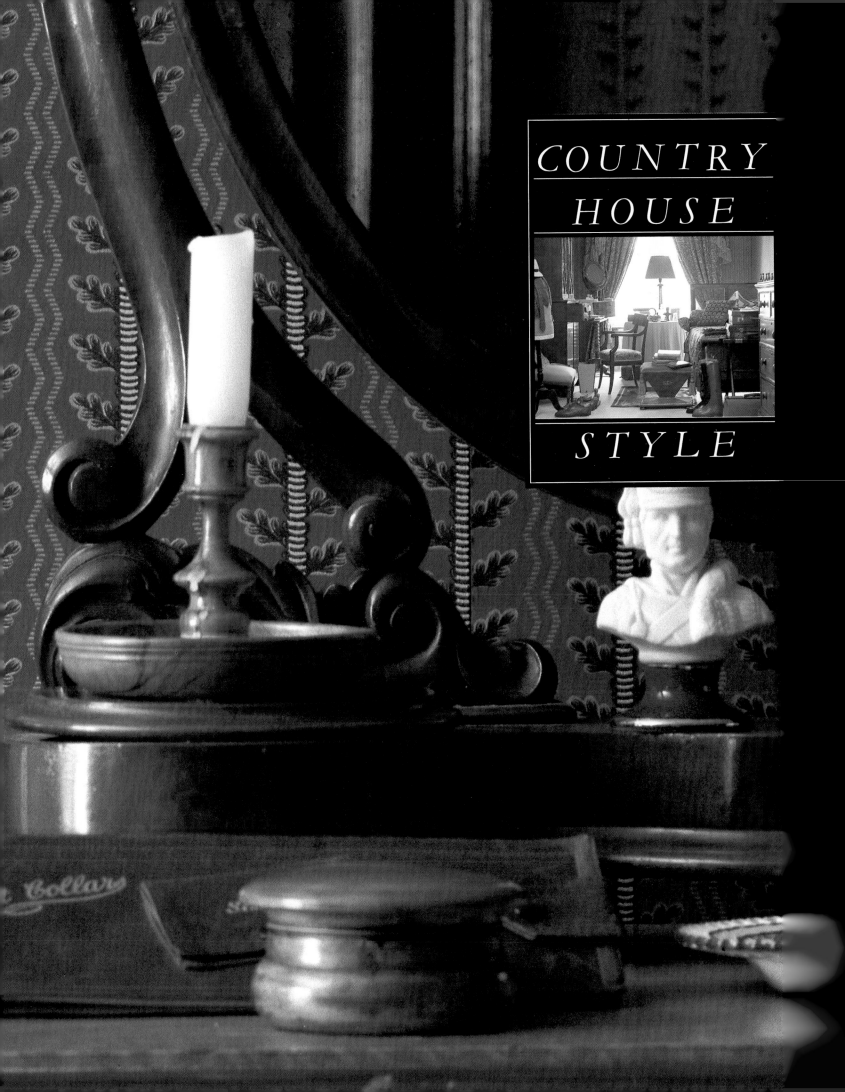

COUNTRY
HOUSE

STYLE

COUNTRY HOUSE STYLE
Past Traditions

The country house and its interior in its most loved form is uniquely English. The very phrase 'country house' conjures up a myriad of familiar images from the glassy elegance of a Gainsborough painting to the endearing eccentricities of the novels of P. G. Wodehouse, in which a dynastic pageant of bucolic earls, rakish younger sons and 'bright young things' spend their days in a variety of traditional country pursuits.

Evelyn Waugh encapsulated the classic aura of the country house in *Brideshead Revisited*: 'It was an aesthetic education to live within those walls, to wander from room to room, from the Soanesque library to the Chinese drawing room, adazzle with gilt pagoda and nodding mandarins, painted paper and Chippendale fretwork, from the Pompeiian parlour to the great tapestry-hung hall which stood unchanged, as it had been designed two hundred and fifty years before . . .'

Today, the style of decoration associated with the country house is still typified by an eclectic profusion, lovingly assembled over the years. But it is no longer a set piece of overwhelming grandeur and aesthetic excellence; rather it is a style that exudes an air of comfort and ease, of faded glory and family memorabilia, and above all of quiet good taste□

Crewel work was a typical pastime of the country house lady throughout the sixteenth and seventeenth centuries. In this charming example of the craft, an abstract flamestitch pattern, similar to that which originated in Italy in the fourteenth century, is used to great effect.

BELOW RIGHT *The Long Gallery at Hardwick Hall, Derbyshire, shown here in a nineteenth-century watercolour by David Cox, provides a fine example of major new features of interior design during the reign of Elizabeth I. The gallery was an English development of the continental covered walkway, raised from the ground to the first floor and glazed the length of the outside wall. It was their enormous scale that made these great galleries such an achievement, providing the inhabitants with a place of recreation away from the notoriously inclement English weather – a room in which to exhibit pictures and* objets d'art, *and which could even serve as a gigantic spare bedroom or theatre.*

BELOW *During the seventeenth century the art of woodcarving, which had been undervalued for centuries, was resurrected by Grinling Gibbons and taken to unprecedented heights. Gibbons combined Baroque exuberance with complete naturalism in pieces such as this panel from Petworth in Sussex. Examples of his art adorn the staircases, panelling and chimneypieces of houses throughout England, notably at Ham House and Windsor Castle.*

In the Middle Ages, the Great Hall of the medieval manor was the indisputable focus of country house life. Nowadays, such halls may look bleak and unwelcoming, but there is considerable evidence that they would have been brilliantly painted, either with colour washes or stencils, and filled with heraldic banners and hunting trophies. The heating of such vast spaces – the Roman system of under-floor central heating had been lost in the Dark Ages – posed quite a problem, and consequently the lord and lady of the manor spent most of their time in the solar, a luxury bed-sitting room adjacent to the hall, containing the more elaborate furnishings of the manor. Window glass was regarded as a moveable element that would have been replaced with painted wooden shutters when the lord and lady were not in residence. Floors were not usually made up of the bare wooden boards or stone flagging we see today; instead, many manor houses were paved with intricately patterned tiles.

The Influence of the Continent

In the sixteenth century, when Italy and France were deeply immersed in the symmetry and splendour of the Renaissance, and the revival of the classical ideals of harmony and balance, the English interior had a somewhat fragmented appearance – but change was on its way. In new houses like Hampton Court, home of Henry VIII, the Great Hall was replaced by a long gallery on the first floor, which was used for recreation and as an official reception room. Here the finest treasures were displayed: furniture was mostly made of oak, with perhaps some cedar or walnut, and was boldly carved or inlaid with ivory, tortoiseshell or mother-of-pearl. The garden, too, showed Renaissance

influence in its geometrical arrangement of architectural vistas. At Audley End in Essex, seat of the Earl of Suffolk, the decorative work of Flemish craftsmen was employed to great effect, while chimneypieces and doorways were modelled on examples from Renaissance textbooks.

Seen against this tradition of interior decoration, the revolutionary achievement of the first significant English architect Inigo Jones (1573–1652) seems all the more remarkable. The son of a humble Smithfield clothworker, Jones had been a designer of masques at the court of James I, travelling to France and Italy in the course of his work. Whilst on the continent he had been impressed by the architectural designs of the Italian architect Andrea Palladio, whose work was to exert a lasting influence on the appearance of the English country house.

On his return to England, Jones set about putting Palladian principles into practice, bringing with him a new sense of harmony and proportion. Features such as temple porticos and circular stairwells became a part of the architectural scene, with elegant classical lines predominating.

In 1660, after the turbulence of the Civil War and Cromwell's Commonwealth, England found herself with a monarch who had spent his years of exile in France and who returned to his new kingdom with French manners and tastes, not least in interior decoration. For the next two hundred years, France was to be a continuing source of inspiration for British design and architecture.

Charles II was concerned that the restored House of Stuart should emulate the Baroque magnificence of the French court of Louis XIV, the Sun King. It was a style designed to impress – and oppress. Beneath an ornate setting of damask hangings, gilded plasterwork, garlands, swags and *putti*, Louis XIV attempted to exercise his God-given power: Charles wanted the same atmosphere, the same backdrop for his kingship, and he modelled the plan and decoration of the royal apartments at Windsor along French lines, creating an elaborate succession of receiving rooms which reflected the complex hierarchy that underpinned court life. Beyond a symbolically grandiose portico lay a large hall, the *grand salon*, where dinner was held, after which guests would retire to the withdrawing room, while the king's intimates would be admitted to an audience in the State Bedchamber. The Great Hall was no longer the central focus of the household.

In two of the most impressive Baroque buildings in England, Castle Howard in Yorkshire and the Duke of Marlborough's Blenheim Palace, the foundations of English country house style were laid. Designed for the purposes of state, they were in fact huge 'show-houses'. But where did one *live*? Jonathan Swift wrote of Blenheim:

This painting of Queen Charlotte and her children by the society portraitist Johann Zoffany provides a good illustration of the arrangement of a fine lady's bedroom of the 1760s. Before the festoon-hung window is a lace-draped dressing table covered in chintz. On the floor is a sumptuously patterned carpet, and on the left of the picture, bearing a toy drum, a gilded, brocade-upholstered chair. Behind Queen Charlotte, on a pedestal, stands a Chinese figurine before a large wall glass, while through the open door we can see the long panelled hall.

The spacious court, the colonnade,
And mind how wide the hall is made;
The chimneys are so well designed,
They never smoke in any wind:
The galleries contrived for walking,
The windows to retire and talk in;
The council chamber to debate,
And all the rest are rooms of state.
'Thanks, sir,' cried I, 'tis very fine,
But where d'ye sleep, or where d'ye dine?
I find, by all you have been telling,
That 'tis a house, but not a dwelling.

To answer Swift's understandable dilemma, such homes were divided up into three areas: the ceremonial, the domestic and the servants' quarters. For everyday living, when no ceremonial display was required, the family would dine in a small parlour, or even as was the practice in France, in a bedchamber. Within these surroundings of outward pomp, new developments were also taking place in furnishings. More luxurious materials and fabrics became fashionable, mostly imported from France: satins trimmed with elaborate fringes and braids, rich silk damasks for wall and bed hangings, and watered moiré silks for chairs. That archetypal country house feature, the four-poster bed, assumed even more importance with the influence of Versailles. The search for evermore theatrical and opulent effects also extended to plasterwork. The most beautiful aspect of earlier Elizabethan and Jacobean interiors, plasterwork now assumed a more elaborate appearance, partly due to the introduction of a new quick-drying stucco, mounted on wire or wood, which replaced the old mixture of lime and plaster of Paris.

The influence of late Baroque style from France and Italy was to be a short-lived period in the history of the English country house. In the early eighteenth century there was a strong reaction (of which Swift's poem is typical) against the European extravagance associated with such architectural projects as Blenheim in favour of the more modest and 'unaffected' style introduced by Inigo Jones, which was regarded by the Whig aristocracy as more honestly English.

Classical Restraint

The year 1715 proved to be a turning point: the first volume of Scottish architect Colen Campbell's satirical attack on Baroque excess, *Vitruvius Britannicus*, was published, as was the first English translation of Palladio's *I quattro libri dell' architettura*, which has been called the most influential architectural book ever written. Both these works had great

impact on that patron of the arts, Richard, Earl of Burlington, who was instrumental in restoring the English country house to its earlier classical form.

Classical Romanticism

The established taste for Palladianism prepared the way for the next change in architectural and design style that was to sweep through the country house: Neo-classicism. This was a style inspired partly by the excavations at Pompeii and Herculaneum, which gave sensational evidence of the reality of classical interiors and buildings, and partly by the purity of Greek taste.

The leading lights of this new trend were two Scotsmen, William Chambers (1723–92) and Robert Adam (1728–92). Chambers was something of a magpie, picking up details and ideas on his travels to such faraway places as China, and extending his influence on design through the publication in 1759 of his *Treatise on Civil Architecture*. Between 1757 and 1763, he laid out the Royal Botanical Gardens at Kew, and in 1769 he designed the delightful interior of Peper Harow in Surrey, which shows many Neo-classical details such as Greek acanthus leaves, lyres and Egyptian sphinxes, all of which were drawn from authentic sources.

One of Burlington's most gifted protégés was William Kent (1685–1748), who has some claim to the title of the first great English interior designer. He developed a distinctive style of country house interior, simple in construction yet ornate in decoration. His Painted

William Kent was one of the most brilliant exponents of English Palladian style in the eighteenth century. Ditchley Park in Oxfordshire demonstrates Kent's facility for creating sumptuous interiors within a framework of classical architecture, using rich stucco-work, painted decoration, carved and gilded wood and vast marble chimneypieces.

This section through a house, drawn in 1774 by John Yenn, a pupil of Sir William Chambers, demonstrates quite clearly the layout and decorative schemes for a grand house of the period. The ground floor contains the reception rooms with their high ceilings and Neo-classical decoration. On the first floor are the principle bedroom and an informal reception room, while the two smaller bedrooms are situated on the third floor, decorated with smart striped wallpaper. Finally, in the attic are the servants' rooms, covered with a lining paper of gingham check.

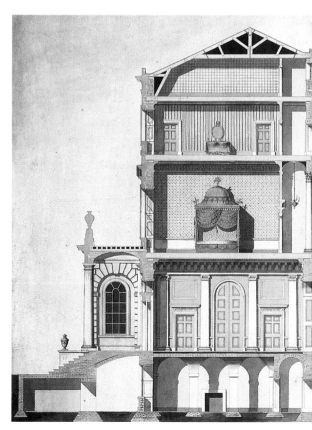

Parlour at Rousham House, Oxfordshire, embodies the freshness and grace of the new manner. He was also a pioneer of the revolt against the formal, enclosed garden in favour of idealized landscaped parkland, while the introduction of the 'ha-ha' – a concealed sunken wall so called because of the element of surprise in coming across it – further effected the integration of house and landscape.

This was also the age of the Grand Tour. Souvenirs gathered by young Englishmen on their travels in Europe filled cabinets of curios on their return: paintings, books, porcelain and jewellery turned the English country house into a treasure trove of artefacts from other ages and cultures.

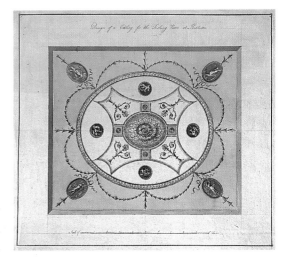

Robert Adam was probably the most important of the English country house decorators of the eighteenth century. Also well travelled, he studied in both Paris and Rome, developing a somewhat picturesque approach to Neo-classicism through his contact with the architect Charles-Louis Clérisseau and the engraver Giambattista Piranesi. Back in England, he set up a partnership with his brother James, and announced his aim to replace the English architectural vices of 'massive entablature, the ponderous compartment ceiling, the tabernacle frame' with a 'beautiful variety of light mouldings, gracefully formed and delicately enriched . . . in the beautiful spirit of antiquity.'

Adam was essentially an interior designer rather than an architect, converting existing country houses in keeping with contemporary

A characteristic feature of Robert Adam's designs was his innovative use of colour, coupled with the reinterpretation of Classical motifs. In these two examples of his work, a ceiling design for the Fishing Room and a design for the Book Room, both from Kedleston Hall in Derbyshire, we can see how Adam took the 'grotesqueries' which he had discovered on his Italian visits of the 1750s and '60s and applied them, in stucco, to his decorative schemes.

tastes. Delicacy was his keynote, both in colour (pastel shades of pale green, blue and pink were characteristic) and in ornament (the coved ceiling of the saloon at Saltram House in Devon is delicately plastered with swags, palmettes, griffins and inset roundels). He also originated the fanciful 'Etruscan' style of decoration, which was used to dazzling effect at Osterley Park in Middlesex.

Gradually, the pioneering tastes of the aristocracy reached more modest landowners. Painted walls replaced wooden panelling, and English or Oriental woven carpets covered the floor, their designs echoing those of the ceilings above. The eighteenth century also saw the increased use of chintz, that most English of fabrics, while the classic arrangement of drawing room, dining room and library came to replace the formal saloon, drawing room and bedchamber.

A Desire for Novelty

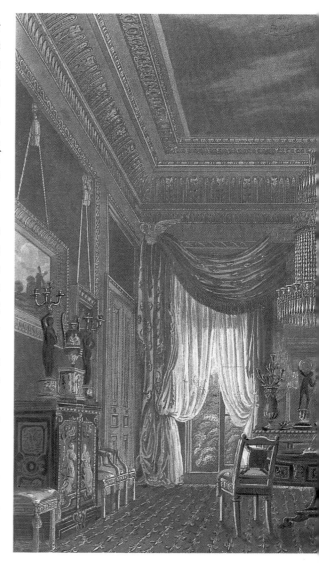

The tide turned again at the end of the eighteenth century: a younger generation now criticized Adam for his 'filigrane toy-work', and there was a thirst for novelty manifested in the vogue for more unusual styles such as chinoiserie and the Gothick. Outside, this taste for the picturesque manifested itself in the Chinese pagodas and Gothic ruins that sprang up in the grounds of country houses. England was in a state of turmoil caused by the French Revolution and the Napoleonic Wars, culminating in the Battle of Waterloo in 1815. Yet despite this state of flux, one can trace certain persistent themes in country house decoration throughout the period.

Classical lines continued to dominate architecture, but what had once appeared graceful and interesting to the eye now looked monotonous and box-like. Decorative details were frequently gilded against a white or tinted ground, or picked out in light relief, and marbling effects were widely used. Large mirrors created an opulent air and candelabra hung from shallow-coffered ceilings. Doors were built high and wide, often double. Around 1800, furniture acquired a more upholstered look: sofas with fitted bolsters and cushions, tasselled and fringed, now made an appearance. Walls were papered, or lined with silk, and rooms were thickly draped and carpeted. For all the basic architectural austerity, there was a compensating taste for sumptuous clutter: drawing rooms were filled with ottomans, chaises longues and domed clocks.

The Regency period, which lasted from 1811 to 1820, was characterized by a desire to link house and garden by means of French windows, opening either into glass conservatories or directly onto a garden or terrace. The Regent's own palace at Carlton House, London, was the perfect example of this fashion.

A taste for the Orient, in particular China, had begun to influence the English country house style of decoration as early as the 1740s. It was usually confined to details, or simple pieces of furniture, although a few rooms did exist furnished entirely in the Chinese taste complete with fine wallpapers. Having been swamped by Neo-classicism during the 1760s and 1770s, this vogue now surfaced in spectacular form with the Prince Regent's pavilion in Brighton in 1816.

The next generation represented the beginning of the era known as 'Victorian'. The prevailing mood of the age was expansive, hopeful, materialistic and affluent. New wealth aped the old aristocracy: merchants, tradesmen and industrialists now saw the possession of a country house as the passport to higher social status, and a great spate of building followed in styles which embodied the solid, comfort-loving values and standards of a new rich bourgeoisie.

The Victorians took themselves very seriously. The Regency was regarded as a period of unprincipled decadence and a moralizing tone permeated architecture, decoration and furnishings as if to symbolize Victorian high-mindedness. One of the most popular styles was that of 'baronial' Gothic, with connotations of an age of chivalry and feudalism when society was strictly structured and belief in Church and King was unquestioned.

The illusion of antiquity also played a part in the *nouveau riche* pretension. The style was well summed up by Evelyn Waugh in his novel *A Handful of Dust* (1934), when he describes a grim Gothic mansion built in 1864:

> . . . the ecclesiastical gloom of the great hall, its ceiling groined and painted in diapers of red and gold, supported on shafts of polished granite with vine-wreathed capitals half-lit by day through lancet windows of armorial stained glass, at night by a vast gasolier of brass and wrought iron . . . the dining hall with its hammer-beam roof and pitch-pine minstrels' gallery; the bedrooms with their brass bedsteads, each with a frieze of Gothic text . . .

Other styles of decoration made their appearance in the mid-Victorian period. Baronial Gothic led to the 'Jacobethan' revival, exemplified by Mentmore House in Buckinghamshire, which was built by Joseph Paxton in 1852. Another theme was a very free treatment of the Italianate Renaissance style, incorporating classical features without adhering to any one source. Typical of this style was Osborne House on the Isle of Wight, designed for Queen Victoria by Prince Albert in collaboration with Thomas Cubitt, and Thomas Hope's Deepdene. There was also a certain vogue for the era of Louis XIV, stimulated by Baron Ferdinand de Rothschild, who commissioned the building of Waddesdon in Buckinghamshire, a full-scale reproduction of an early eighteenth-century French chateau complete with mansard roof, period panelling and elaborately gilded furniture.

Whatever the exterior style, the interior of the Victorian country house was consistently filled with heavily upholstered furniture, deeply padded, quilted and rounded, with a profusion of fringing and trimming. In general, decorative treatments became less subtle, the line heavier. Wallpaper was densely floral, large clocks appeared on mantelpieces and embroidered screens stood by the fire.

The Paisley pattern now became popular. This was a vogue that had in fact started in the late eighteenth century, when travellers to India had returned with beautiful, hand-woven shawls from Kashmir. So sought after were they that the East India Company started to import them. A weaver in Edinburgh decided to copy these shawls less expensively by using mass production, and he set up his factory in the Scottish town of Paisley in 1805. The pine cone motif appeared not just on furnishing fabrics but also woollen shawls for ladies, worn throughout Europe and America over voluminous crinolines.

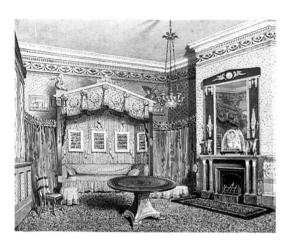

The extremities of Regency opulence are well illustrated in the Small Drawing Room at The Deepdene in Surrey, home of Thomas Hope. The influence of Empire style, imported from Napoleon's France, is deeply felt here, particularly in the draped sofa, ornate chimneypiece and instantly arresting salmon pink colour scheme. All the details of the room, down to the exact colour tone, would have been to Hope's own precise specifications.

The prints of that important nineteenth-century designer Owen Jones were also a feature of the Victorian country house: Gothic revival trellis patterns and classical acanthus motifs were used with geometric patterns derived from Greek precedents. Jones's love of Islamic and Moorish decoration, as well as oriental and primitive art, influenced his own stylized designs. Placed in charge of the decoration of the Crystal Palace, his influence was felt in all branches of the decorative arts during the second half of the nineteenth century.

The accumulated collections of small *objets d'art* and artefacts were evident everywhere, from shell mosaics to leather-bound or hand-painted scrapbooks, vases in exotic shapes and brilliant glazes, sewing boxes and bric-a-brac – much of it useless, but all of it cherished with sentimental intensity and displayed lovingly on whatnots or in glass-fronted cabinets. The art of taxidermy brought a stuffed animal into every hall or passage, and preserved loved and lost pets. At its best, it could be an Aladdin's cave of treasures, redolent of warmth and comfort; at its worst, it was damp, stuffy and oppressive.

At the end of the nineteenth century, attitudes to the country house style in America were redefined. In 1897, the future novelist Edith Wharton, together with architect Ogden Codman, published a volume on interiors, *The Decoration of Houses*. It made the vital distinction between upholsterer and decorator and went on to criticize the vulgarity of American taste, advocating the 'French way' of decoration as the new standard to be followed by an eager public. This represents an important moment in the retreat from the sumptuary excesses of the late Victorian era and a resumption of the curvaceous elegance of the eighteenth century. Edith Wharton's decorator, Elsie de Wolfe, succeeded in putting this trend into commercial practice, executing triumphant schemes of 'old French' interiors for the wealthy Frick family in New York.

ABOVE *Knightshayes Court, designed by William Burges in 1867, provides an excellent example of the sort of imaginative fantasy which characterized much of the country house architecture and decoration of the second half of the nineteenth century. Burges was the epitome of the medievalizing architect.*

BELOW *Originally an Indian design, based on the pine cone motif, the paisley pattern takes its name from the town in Scotland which produced these fabrics and shawls to satisfy an ever increasing demand.*

At the same time in England, Edwin Lutyens (1869–1944) was beginning to establish a new style of country house which managed to escape the Victorian revivalist clichés, while combining the best of the Arts and Crafts attention to detail with classical proportions. From the granite masses of Castle Drogo in Devon to the more modest Queen Anne symmetry of The Salutation in Sandwich, Lutyens showed himself a masterly interpreter of the new country house tradition, creating austere yet subtle interiors, unafraid of bare stone and plaster, and liberated from the pieties of Pugin. Nor did he baulk at the audacious and even humorous: at Marshcourt in Hampshire, he built a billiard table out of one huge piece of local chalk, and a circular nursery, which meant that no child could ever be put in the corner.

The chief preoccupations of the Victorian owner of a country house would have included health, manifesting itself in an obsession with drains, sewerage and ventilation; and the hierarchical segregation of ages and classes leading to maze-like interiors in which rooms and staircases were visibly and distinctively graded. There was still little idea of how to circulate and conserve heat effectively and economically, except via a stove or fireplace, and bathrooms with running water were not considered an essential part of everyday life. A servant would be summoned to bring up a bathtub, placed next to the bedroom fire, which would then be filled from kettles and jugs. The great Victorian prima donna Adelina Patti, whose baronial Gothic mansion of Craig-y-nos, near Swansea, was considered the last word in luxurious modernity (it even had electric burglar alarms), only felt it necessary to have three bathrooms to serve thirty-four bedrooms.

Throughout all these developments the only element to remain constant was a love of the countryside. The rising middle classes may not have been able to acquire the country mansion to which they all aspired, but at least on their fashionably papered walls they could hang images of such houses alongside landscapes and 'ancestral' portraits of dubious provenance. The Queen herself had a taste for the countryside, in particular the Highlands of Scotland, and such was her all-pervading influence that mansion and villa alike reflected this theme.

The Country House in Peril

After the First World War, traditional country house style was overtaken by a rush of romantic revivalism. There was an anxiousness to forget the nightmare of the past and move on to something new. Yet the aristocracy seemed desperate to hang on to the last shreds of their power and standing. What was universal was the reaction against Victorian heaviness and pomposity: one of the problems in the marriage between Tony and Brenda Last in Waugh's *A Handful of Dust*

America in the 1890s saw a rediscovery of the linear elegance that had characterized interior decoration during the eighteenth century. The sombre, over-stuffed look of the high-Victorian era was rejected in favour of what was now termed the 'Old French' style of light, pale colours and curvilinear furniture. By the early 1900s this style had achieved popularity in Europe, and by 1910, when this watercolour was painted to advertise the services of a furniture manufacturer in the North of England, it was being widely imitated throughout fashionable society. Here, half-panelled walls are hung with pink silk damask, complemented by the light green of the drapery with its delicate muslin or lace inner curtain. The ubiquitous screen makes an appearance, with an almost Art Nouveau 'S' curve to its top, while the central focus of the room is the piano, without which no Edwardian interior would have been complete.

is Tony's fossilized attachment to his cold, gloomy white elephant of a house, opposed by Brenda's longing for a flat with 'bedroom, bath and telephone ... constant hot water and central heating ... white chromium plating and natural sheepskin carpet.'

Brenda lives in the world of the modern interior decorator. The most famous firms were Lenygon's, which specialized in 'comfortable Georgian' – Loelia, Lady Lindsay of Dowhill, described their trademark as the 'invariably panelled drawing room, painted a colour halfway between blue and green' – and the partnership of Sybil Colefax and John Fowler, whose principle was freedom 'from too many rules ... a sense of graciousness ... mannered, yet casual and unselfconscious.'

Another style, avidly taken up by the aristocracy at this time, was that of 'trans-atlantic luxury', propagated by the interior decorator Mrs Syrie Maugham. It contains a touch of the Neo-classical, a hint of Louis XIV, and a flavour of the film set. Characterized by glass lamps, large mirrors, pink silks and green satins, and monochrome fitted carpets, it was a style acidly described by the novelist and critic Peter Quennell:

> With off-white upholstery went pickled oak side tables and baroque accessories denuded of the paintwork they demanded and deserved. Such an interior was smart, chilly, entirely impractical, and for many reasons, including the gullibility of the rich and the ingenuity of fashionable interior decorators, extraordinarily expensive.

In 1939, with the outbreak of the Second World War, the country house entered another period of peril. Many were requisitioned for a variety of wartime uses: some became barracks for the military (Waugh's Brideshead, for one), others were used as hospitals and convalescent homes, schools for evacuated children or storage depots for works of art. Many owners despaired of recovering their homes even when peace had been restored. A number had been seriously damaged, with old plasterwork and panelling ripped out; others had suffered severe bomb damage. In addition, new legislation, which raised the taxation on the aristocracy, reduced the funds available for restoring such houses to their former glory. The country house and everything it represented appeared to be doomed. Indeed, in Waugh's preface to the 1960 edition of his novel *Brideshead Revisited* he admitted 'it seemed then that the ancestral seats which were our chief national artistic achievement were doomed to decay and spoliation like the monasteries in the sixteenth century.'

The Country House Restored

Fortunately, while the twentieth century has been a period of dispersal and destruction, it has also been a time of restoration. Throughout the 1950s and 1960s, there was a change of attitude towards England's heritage and the many pasts of the country house were lovingly and painstakingly resurrected, influencing taste and fashion in decoration in both England and America. 'Country house style' has developed from being fashionable among a favoured few to becoming a popular look that can be applied to a variety of environments. The main achievement of the post-war period lay in re-opening country houses to the public, with the consequent need to redecorate, and gardens were restored in keeping with such houses. A strong element of curiosity about the way in which people lived gave rise to great enthusiasm for country house visiting, and patterns of the past have become a strong inspiration for present day living.

The country house style was taken up by Laura Ashley in the 1980s, a natural successor and complement to the rustic style which had become so popular throughout the 1960s and 1970s. Richer colours were used with greater daring and understanding; cotton, no longer a 'cottagey' fabric, was given greater sophistication with the application of prints on a larger scale and the introduction of chintz and a heavier weight cotton satin. Interiors had a characteristic timelessness that appeared natural and effortless but which was achieved with considerable attention to detail. The comfort of unfussy sofas and chairs, the use of flowers and plants, made a certain formality acceptable. Classic designs and colours were revived to bring out the harmonious proportions of a room, establishing a unity and balance with added emphasis given to dados and cornices.

With its aura of comfort and ease, its sense of tradition and past associations, English country style is at home all over the world.

A drapery design from a Parisian decorator demonstrates the 'Old French' style of the 1900s. With its ornate fringing, tie-backs, separate draped pelmet and co-ordinating blind, it clearly draws on Pierre de la Mesangère's influential designs of a century earlier.

COUNTRY HOUSE STYLE
Laura Ashley

For Laura Ashley, the essence of country house style is a sense of comfort and tranquility. A country house is a relaxing retreat where formality, perhaps even grandeur, is unselfconsciously blended with the happy practicalities of family life. It is not a set piece of design theory but a living environment evolving in time through loving use.

This sense of naturalness and ease is in fact achieved through careful and extensive research. Inspiration for fabric and wallpaper designs was sought out in the daily life of the past, in the attics and storerooms of the country houses of England, in historic archives and in treasured scraps of antique chintz and muslin. Laura Ashley's own paisley and chinoiserie patterns reflect the traditional eclecticism of country house style, while full-blown floral chintzes echo the glories of the outside world.

It is this feeling for the past, a respect for tradition and a love of the countryside that together form the key to the rich mellowness of colour and texture that characterizes the country house interior, that sense of timeless dependability which can infuse the most far-flung or metropolitan home with something of the spirit of the English country house that has been its inspiration □

Country house style is about having the hauteur to call your living room a drawing room and then the nonchalance to put gilded tables next to Great Aunt Agatha's threadbare, buttonback sofa. Breathtaking proportions, grand ideas, the accumulation of centuries of different styles, all are consolidated by the genius for eclecticism which is English chic. This stone-flagged and panelled room near Bath in Wiltshire shows that particular mix of the magisterial and informal which has made the English country house one of the most copied looks in the world.

Bed curtains came long before window curtains, so why abandon them now? Originally, their function was to keep out draughts, but this has been gradually superseded by their superb decorative possibilities. Singlehandedly they can transform a bedroom from the ordinary to the sumptuous. Nor need they be incompatible with a modern bed, as here, where an elegant headcloth and canopy frame the bedhead. A restrained single swag falls in loose folds above, and narrow side curtains are caught back below mattress level. The head-cloth is of gently-pleated cowslip cotton, shadowed with a faint pattern. Hanging a print and silhouettes within this space lends a formal note and adds to the overall boldness of the statement.

The windows have a chorus of curtains which repeat the single swag of the canopy over each window, and a paper border continues the theme of roses right round the room. The ebullience of the rose-strewn chintz is complemented by posies on the wallpaper and a similar print on bolster, quilt and bedhead, intensified with a lattice pattern. The checked, smoke-fringed tablecloth is a stabilizing influence, subtly emphasized by the criss-cross of the lattice on the bed. A rug by the sofa takes the floral image in a different direction with a stylized *faux* needlework pattern played up by the needlework on the sewing-box lid.

Dining has always been a highly ceremonious occasion, and often requires a sober and sumptuous setting to suit. This English dining room is in the country house tradition of rich colours and heavy, dark furniture. It gleams with the lustre of dark wood, old oil paintings, silver, china and candles. The unexpectedly light, wide-striped wallpaper is a marvellous foil for the rich tints of curtains, sideboards and upholstery. The curtains are made up in a satin-weave cotton which emulates the cotton sateen beloved of the Victorians. It has a soft, natural drape and is enriched with a dense, vivid pattern of foliage on a navy ground. Paisley cushions and the deep but muted colours of tartan rugs are part of the same design vocabulary.

On the table, a glazed chintz buttermilk tablecloth acts as a foil to dark colours in the same way as the wallpaper. It is dressed up with a bullion fringe in burgundy to match the chair seats, and has a pragmatic function in covering the more formal cloth, matching the curtains, which peeps out beneath. The table is laid with a bucolic breakfast for a riding party, with tablemats in a burgundy and navy pattern taken from a print by the Victorian designer Owen Jones. The candlesticks sport the diminutive 'hats' popular before the Second World War and still to be seen in the more old-fashioned Oxford colleges. The dining chairs are upholstered in soft, but hard-wearing, burgundy leather.

This drawing room in the grand manner nevertheless has a relaxed, lived-in feel provided by details like the crowded objects on the mantelpiece and desk, a jumble of pretty cushions, and the tassel-edged throw rug that breaks up the lines of the sofa. A sense of breadth and dignity is established in the overall treatment of the room. The proportions are the first consideration – tall, spacious and with long, elegant windows. Finely-executed French panelling gives a noble aspect to the room, and does not need to be over-emphasized. It is gently picked out in sand against a light but quiet sage-green background. Surfaces are of marble and glowing wood, and deeply fringed and tasselled curtains are hung Empire-style with a swagged pelmet. Above the fireplace is the mirror essential to a stately sense of space.

Details are suggestive of a civilized existence: the globe, an alabaster bust on a plinth, old oil paintings on the walls, statuettes here and there, leather-bound books. But this is not carried too far; it is quite casual, and the oils, for instance, are hung unframed from big blue taffeta bows. A club-like atmosphere emanates from details like the wooden spine for the newspaper and the paw-footed ottoman, its bulky outline given a more pleasing sense of proportion with a bullion fringe.

Cleverly mismatched pattern is used to break up any too formal overtones; at the same time a limited colour range of sage, sand and subdued blue controls the air of superior calm.

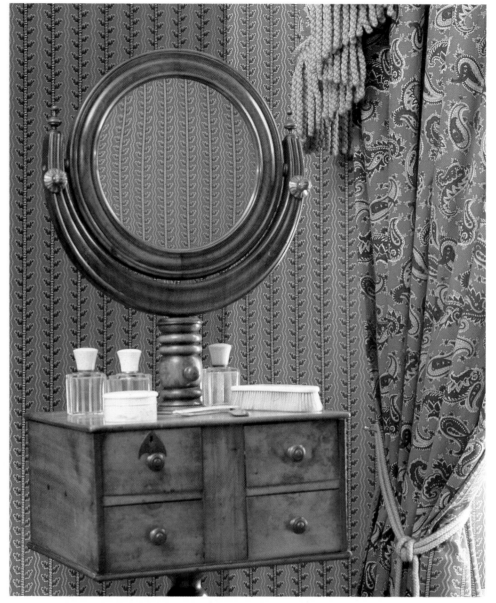

In a country house of the last century the dressing room was the inner sanctum where a gentleman retired to dress, doze or write letters. The same sense of the grand manner, tempered with a casual masculine clutter, has been re-created in this Englishman's apartment in Belgium using fine, deep colours and strong patterns.

A warm, intimate atmosphere is established with a burgundy and tan colour scheme. The walls are papered with a smart linear pattern of oakleaves, taken from a nineteenth-century dress print. The same print lines the heavily fringed paisley curtains which impose a sense of decorum and stateliness. A swagged pelmet is decorated with a rope trim while the curtains are pulled back with tasselled ropes. Paisley also embellishes bed, bolster and chair seat. Everywhere the gleam of burnished leather and wood adds to the air of well-bred informality.

The dressing room has the further luxury of a bathroom leading off it. A decorative link is established with the continued dominance of the paisley motif and colours taken from the dressing room. The magnificent bath is tented in imitation of a medieval example spotted in an English castle, the drapes culminating in a gilded corona. The stencilled frieze was inspired by a Victorian bath designed by the Armitage company. A festoon blind, normally considered a feminine flamboyance, is transformed by a six-inch navy bullion fringe. All the woodwork is smartened with navy paint, and a navy *faux* braid border.

This classic English breakfast room has a sense of solidity imposed by the bold outlines of dark wood against a pretty, smoke-coloured trellis wallpaper. The triple bay windows are emphasized in this way, unadorned apart from the original oak and mahogany shutters and pale striped sunblinds. Consequently the room takes full advantage of the morning light. Instead of a curtain, a great swag of cloth is wound loosely over the curtain pole that fronts the bay. Similar to the wallpaper, but embellished with central rose stems, it was adapted from an 1840s English furnishing fabric. The side window is hung with an equally informal drape of the same cloth.

The floor is left bare and smoothly polished, and an oak refectory table reflects the dark oak of the panelling. The solid, square-shaped dining chairs are covered in cowslip cotton, simply attached with brass tacks. Above, the globe of a Georgian brass chandelier echoes the carved table legs with its well-rounded shape.

Window seats provide quiet corners for catnapping and reading the morning papers. They are covered in a brisk club check with cushions to match the curtains. A Queen Anne armchair is upholstered in a subtle two-toned cowslip print that matches the dining chairs. The table is laid for breakfast, always an informal meal. Cottage loaf, eggs and fruit are presented in rough-cast country pottery, pewter, wooden bowls and earthenware.

The study is a traditionally masculine retreat. Nowadays, of course, women enjoy its quiet, relaxing and bookish charms at least as much as men. In this writer's study in the country, a texture-patterned wallpaper in jade is used for the walls, a cool but definite colour which emphasizes the feeling of privacy. It contrasts smartly with the cream coloured cornice, fireplace and the area below the dado rail. The same shade is used in subtle ways to unify the room: for the fringe that edges the curtains and pelmet, and for a chintz cushion or two. It is also picked out in the floral print used for remaining cushions and curtains.

A desk sits in the bay, fully armed for action with its period typewriter and telephone, still in working order. (Its Williamsburg counterpart, above left, has a more colonial air.) The armchair and Snowdon sofa are of the kind that are bliss to sink into, with loose covers in a subdued terracotta print, taken from Queen Anne style needlework. The mantel is decorated in classic drawing room fashion with a mirror and pair of candlesticks, but other, more eccentric objects add humour and a sense of personal idiosyncrasy. A 'Roman' bust in the fireplace is a reminder of the marble and plaster heads which adorn more learned libraries, a station clock ticks lugubriously in one corner, and in another a harmonium is provided for playing music when inspiration fails. The bookcases with bays of jade paintwork have been specially made for the owner's collection. Books do indeed furnish a room, especially beautiful leatherbound volumes such as these.

'Less pose than French taste, more subtle than English', was how Mrs Haweis described the American appropriation of country house style in 1882. This Florida house was designed at the turn of the century by a follower of Addison Mizner. Mizner was much influenced by Spanish and Italian architecture, and in his interiors Spanish features are fused with French refinement and English ease on a grand scale, resulting in rooms of confident originality which also look completely natural.

What first marks this drawing room as non-English are the sun-baked Spanish tiles, with big pots of hydrangeas emphasizing the alfresco feel. The panelling is a singular development from the heavy oak of old England. Bleached boards of pecky cypress (so called because it looks as though a giant bird has pecked it) line the walls, with mouldings placed straight over the undisguised planks. Against this background play elements of French frivolity – sugar-icing gilt tables, pink marble, an ornate desk and commode, a lustre-drop chandelier, a Cupid bearing candles aloft – and a solid, unpretentious Englishness which comes through in the formality of the curtains, the comfort of sofa and armchair, and the touches of chinoiserie, a well-loved English theme especially in the eighteenth century.

The key to succeeding with such a room is in pulling the threads of the different styles together. An unusual precedent has been set here by using a small detail, the chinoiserie cushions, as the inspiration for the colour scheme of the whole room: buttermilk and smoke blue.

The nursery is completely different from any other room in a country house. Scaled-down for children it takes on an appropriate change of taste from the handsome and grand to the light-hearted and pretty. But there is the same accumulation of old, cherished things, this time great-great-grandmother's Victorian dolls and paper elephant, mixed with battered bears and a modern rag doll.

Yet it is not out of keeping with the rest of the house. Several of the broad strokes of style from downstairs are sketched in a fresher, more playful character upstairs. The great, floor-sweeping curtains caught back with twisted satin cords are here quaintly reduced to window size, but have tie-backs nevertheless, and a pert, pink-piped bow in place of festive loops and swags. The magnificent beds on the floor below are echoed in the stately structure of the Victorian cot, which is painted white and given the Sleeping Beauty drapes of a *lit polonaise*. The cloth, with twirly stripes of smoke blue dividing up the pink nosegays, is from an eighteenth-century French *toile*, and makes an elegant fabric for curtains and drapes. Using the same pattern for the wallpaper brings a humble reminder of a cottage parlour. The rose pink in this print is pulled out for the simple wickerwork pattern that lines the bed curtains and covers the chair and pillow. The floor repeats the time-honoured flagging design of the country house – not baronial slabs but diamonds, simply stencilled over white-painted boards. The effect is charming.

ROMANTIC

STYLE

ROMANTIC STYLE
Past Traditions

Flowers are always closely linked with all things romantic. Whether the association is of a garden bower, or the fragrance of roses filling a room, the romantic inspiration of flowers can be traced back to the Middle Ages. Flower paintings such as this watercolour of anenomes, executed by John Edwards in 1783, were a decorative feature of the eighteenth-century interior.

A certain undercurrent of romanticism and illusion runs throughout the history of interior decoration, an undercurrent which at intervals surfaces to become the mainstream of design style.

From classical times, there has been a taste for the extravagant, the luxurious and the dramatic. The fantastical decorative conceits of Ancient Rome and Byzantium were very much part of a public image designed to impress and overawe. Artists of the Renaissance turned the latest fashions in ornamental and illusionistic devices to decorative use in the fabulous interiors they painted for the Italian dukes, while the baroque era put romantic style into a grand theatrical setting with evermore complex and ingenious schemes for spectacular fountains, seashell grottos and dazzling mirror rooms – the ultimate illusion. The playful arabesques of the Rococo wove their way across the plasterwork, panelling and furniture of the eighteenth century, later followed by the Gothic visions of a fairy-tale world of battlemented parapets and dream castles.

The twentieth century has seen romantic style take on a lighter, frolicsome, fancy-dress style with the designs of Cecil Beaton and Rex Whistler; decorative schemes have now become the stuff of magic □

An overwhelmingly feminine sense of style emanates from this mid-Victorian bedroom. It reflects all the romantic preoccupations of that period in its profusion of lace, light colours and floral-patterned fabrics.

The story could well begin in the court of a Roman emperor. Little of Nero's monumentally lavish Domus Aurea, or Golden House, remains on the Esquiline Hill in Rome, but accounts of its construction, recorded by various contemporary writers, have survived. Built in the middle of the first century AD, this fantasy rested on a very material improvement in the strength of a form of concrete, which permitted rooms of larger size and more adventurous shape. The Octagon Room, which housed lavish decorative schemes, was one of the wonders of the age. Ceilings of ivory, brightly coloured silks, and gold; ingenious mechanical marvels which enabled one ceiling to revolve producing the illusion of the heavens, with the planets and stars spinning through space; ceilings with pipes that sprinkled perfumes or opened to scatter cascades of flowers on the lounging diners below – these were just some of the special effects that were employed. Decorated by the appropriately named Fabullus, 'who worked without a moment's respite on the Golden House, which became his chosen prison', the Octagon had walls of mosaic and fresco, floors of marble, with finishing touches of gold and mother-of-pearl. Nero's incomparable art collection completed the splendour of the display.

The spirit of the Domus Aurea lived on in the Great Palace of Constantinople, where the Byzantine emperors held sway through the

Dark Ages. From tenth-century accounts we can recapture some of its fabulous glamour. The Emperor himself sat upon a huge and ornate gilded throne which, during an audience, would be whisked away by hidden mechanics high into the air, where it would appear to be suspended, while on either side a pair of mechanical bronze lions would roar and move menacingly. From the ceiling hung chandeliers of solid gold, and gold food bowls too heavy to carry stood upon the table. Upon the floors was strewn an abundance of rose petals and the most exotic building materials imaginable were to be seen everywhere. The walls and ceilings were inlaid with painted glass, precious stones and porphyry, while above the floors of highly polished silver hung draperies of the finest silk.

The Imperial Bedchamber was a breathtaking room in the middle of which stood a fountain, inlaid with semi-precious stones, from which ran four streams of crystal water. The marble walls were pierced with sheets of glass painted with flowers and fruit, while the ceiling was encrusted with mosaics.

Such magnificence has remained legendary. In our own century the poet W. B. Yeats has celebrated the 'hammered gold' of the Byzantine court, and perhaps nothing has ever matched it since, although the great medieval palaces of Arabic Spain, like the Alhambra in Granada with its mosaic walls and glittering fountains, are at least a reflection of its glory.

Painted illusion in the Green Closet at Ham House, Surrey; its coved ceiling is filled with idealized landscapes, putti and garlands.

The Nymphenburg Palace at Amaliensburg is a masterpiece of Rococo romanticism.

Painted Fantasies of the Renaissance

The Renaissance was one of the most romantic periods of interior decoration, providing many of the motifs later taken up by the decorating enthusiasts of years to come. The sophistication of painting techniques and the development of perspective meant that much more could be achieved on flat wall surfaces, without resort to the jewellery and elaborate mechanical devices favoured by the Romans and Byzantines. The frescos painted by Andrea Mantegna for the Ducal Palace at Mantua in 1465–74 show this new style, in which real room space is extended by 'fictional' painted space. Trompe l'oeil curtains of rich crimson damask are drawn back to reveal the landscape of the Veneto and the pageant of the Gonzaga family and their courtiers. Colourful painted garlands hang from the ceiling and painted *putti* gaze down upon the scene, over a delicate balustrade. This elaborate illusionism was to lend the same magical quality to the interiors of the Baroque and Rococo eras.

This decorative tradition was continued in Italy by Giulio Romano, a pupil of Raphael's, in the frescos begun in 1532 for the Sala dei Giganti

or Room of the Giants, in the Palazzo del Te, also in Mantua. The trompe l'oeil architecture opens onto a vision of Mount Olympus: when the painted door is closed, you are entirely lost in the cataclysmic conflict between the Giants of the Earth and the Gods of the Ancient World. All around, the palaces and caves of the giants collapse, seeming to topple inwards, while above, on what is in actuality a low ceiling, the gods ascend in a lofty spiral towards Jupiter's throne.

Baroque Conceits

Throughout the sixteenth and seventeenth centuries, fantastic and whimsical architectural conceits multiplied as the Baroque era encouraged decorators to become ever more complex and ingenious: intricate serpentine patterns and filigree tracery, twisting double staircases, grottos lined with shells and coral and spectacularly engineered fountains.

The grandest of all Baroque fantasies was the vast palace of Louis XIV at Versailles, where Charles Le Brun created a series of sumptuous interiors starting with the Staircase of the Ambassadors and culminating in the Room of Apollo. The most dazzling of all, however, was the Galerie des Glaces or Hall of Mirrors, designed by Le Brun and the architect Hardouin-Mansart in 1678, with its magically glittering counterpoint of mirror and plate glass which seems to turn the elegant formal park outside into a dream image.

The paintings of Watteau, along with those of his contemporaries Fragonard and Boucher, reflect the romantic preoccupations of the Rococo. Here, in a timeless re-creation of a forest glade, Watteau portrays a troubadour playing to his lover at one of the fêtes champêtres *in which the aristocracy of this period frequently indulged.*

This design for a brocaded damask, dating from 1744, provides a good example of the application of the serpentine 'line of beauty' so essential to the Rococo style.

Rococo Enchantment

If the Baroque style represents romantic fantasy as a grand theatrical setting, its successor – the Rococo – represents something much lighter, sweeter and more intimate. It is marked above all by the freely moving line of the arabesque which curls its playful, asymmetrical way round so much wall panelling, plasterwork and furniture of the early eighteenth century. Perhaps the happiest example of a fantasy Rococo interior is the pavilion of the Nymphenburg Palace in Munich, built by François Cuvilliés between 1734 and 1739. The interior is decorated with rich stucco work inset with porcelain, lacquer, mirror glass and fine gilded carving that displays a plethora of natural motifs: flowers, fruits and seashells as well as garlands and ribbons.

The romantic ideal is perfectly summed up in the painting of the Rococo period. The *fêtes galantes* of Fragonard, Watteau, Boucher and Lancret all evoked, in their own ways, the enchanted lands, populated

by figures painted with so light a touch that they often seem to float on a sea of transparent colour. Such paintings would have been inset above doorways, filling the gilded and panelled rooms with an air of pastoral romance.

Gothic Romanticism

The Gothic style has been an underlying trend in romantic design from the mid eighteenth century. Here, at Strawberry Hill in Middlesex, Horace Walpole designed this fanciful ceiling in papier mâché and hung the walls with copies of portraits by Holbein. His bed is set in a recess at the far end of the room, strongly reminiscent of the private solar of the feudal lord of the Middle Ages.

In England, one aspect of Rococo style which was to have a far reaching influence on the future of decorative taste was the Gothic, one of the most potent of architectural and design fantasies. Why, in an age otherwise devoted to Reason and moderation, did this theme capture the imagination? Kenneth Clark attempted an explanation in *The Gothic Revival* (1928):

> Every romantic style reflects the daydream of its creators, some Utopia in which they live the life of the imagination . . . when life is fierce and uncertain the imagination craves for classical repose. But as society becomes tranquil, the imagination is starved of action . . . And Gothic was exotic if not remote in space . . . it had an associative as well as decorative value. Nothing else was so apt to tickle the eighteenth century's jaded palate.

The two eighteenth-century figures whose palates were most demonstrably tickled by Gothic romanticism were Horace Walpole and William Beckford. Walpole's 'villa' at Strawberry Hill, Twickenham, bought as a cottage in 1747, was conceived as a showpiece. The interior featured papier mâché fan vaulting, copied from a medieval ceiling, while the bedroom was hung with mauve wallpaper. For all its 'period' detail, the house was a fanciful pastiche in which classical, chinoiserie and Rococo elements all played a part. 'Charming irregularities' were Walpole's aesthetic aim, and asymmetry was his means of achieving it.

An even more splendid eclectic confusion was William Beckford's Gothic Fonthill Abbey in Wiltshire, a dream palace built between 1796 and 1818 by James Wyatt to Beckford's own designs. His intention was to evoke a medieval abbey. An impressive octagonal room was swathed in mauve drapery, windows were inset with the glowing colours of stained glass showing historical scenes (again, the historical accuracy went no further than a certain visual flavour), the furniture was light French Rococo in style and the most commonly used colour of paint was a very unmonastic shade of pink. Enormous in scale – St Michael's Gallery, for instance, was 127 foot long and 13 foot wide – Fonthill was structurally weak, and the collapse of a 300-foot spire in 1825 led to the eventual demolition of the entire building. Nonetheless, Beckford's Fonthill Abbey represents one man's achievement of his own romantic dream.

Battlemented parapets, pointed windows, sashes and glazing bars, together with an overall lightness and flimsiness of ornament began to appear in a number of mid-eighteenth-century English houses along with a preoccupation with that mythical golden age of chivalry that has characterized aspects of the English decorative arts since Stuart times. A vogue for 'follies' led to all manner of artificial ruins springing up in parks and gardens, completing the romantic landscape.

In France Napoleon had been realizing his own romantic ideals. Having distributed the crowns of his new Europe around the various members of his family, he furnished each of them with a lavishly decorated palace, sparing no expense to create a style of decoration suitable to his own glorious Empire. Queen Hortense had a tented boudoir in pleated blue silk, while in Murat's study in Naples, cascades of filmy lace drapery fell from every window.

The romantic style continued in France in the mid nineteenth century in the art and poetry of the decadents, such as Baudelaire. Romanticism in England was also imbued with a powerfully imaginative literary element which had a deep and long lasting influence on all aspects of taste. The reflection upon harmony between man and nature is the underlying theme of the work of such poets as Wordsworth, Coleridge, Blake, Byron, Shelley and Keats. Against this romantic literary background certain figures stand out in the field of decoration, in particular Sir John Soane, whose most fanciful interior must be that of his own house at Lincoln's Inn Fields, London.

At Fonthill William Beckford outshone even Walpole in the scope of his medieval imaginings. This watercolour of the south end of St Michael's Gallery, decorated in a capricious shade of pink, shows the essence of the Gothic style. A decorative scheme of the present day echoes its eighteenth-century counterpart.

With the end of the Georgian era, Gothic became a more sober matter. For A. W. N. Pugin, the romantic frivolity of houses like Strawberry Hill and Fonthill Abbey became a subject for disapproval, reflecting the more earnest, guilt-ridden face of Victorianism. Perhaps some vestige of the romantic tradition was kept alive in the paintings of the Pre-Raphaelite Brotherhood, whose canvases are peopled with such figures as Ophelia, Lorenzo and Isabella, and themes from Arthurian legend and courtly love.

The modernistic meets the romantic in this Glasgow School interior by George Logan, a contemporary of Charles Rennie Mackintosh. Logan has taken that most romantic of motifs, the rose, and applied it to virtually every available surface in the room. The sinuous lines, muted colours and floral motifs all combine to create an atmosphere quite as romantic as that of Watteau's fête champêtre *of almost two centuries earlier.*

Wagnerian sensuality and decadence dominated late-nineteenth-century culture. Creative energies were channelled into an idealization of beauty, dream and romance, rejecting utterly the values of both the prosperous conventional bourgeoisie and the struggling working class. Art was better than life, artifice more real than reality. Clothe, furnish and surround yourself with fantasy – this was the notion embodied in J. K. Huysman's novel of 1884, *A Rebours*:

The walls he eventually decided to bind like books in large-grained crushed morocco . . . when the lining of the walls had been completed, he had the mouldings and the tall plinths lacquered a deep indigo . . . the ceiling, which was slightly coved, was also covered in morocco; and set in the middle of the orange leather,

like a huge circular window open to the sky, there was a piece of royal blue silk from an ancient cope on which silver seraphim had been depicted in angelic flight by the weavers' guild of Cologne.

Aestheticism and Art Nouveau

This exotic Art Nouveau fabric, dating from 1899, deserves comparison with the elaborate textile designs of the Rococo style. Here are the same arabesque lines, swirling and falling across the print, together with highly stylized plant and bird motifs. The peacocks are immediately redolent of the work of such aesthetes as James McNeill Whistler.

Aestheticism and Art Nouveau were the last two styles of a truly romantic nature before the emergence of the Modern Movement of the 1920s. Whistler's Peacock Room, with its exotic combination of lacquer and silk in rich shades of green and gold is perhaps the finest of aesthetic interiors. The style of Art Nouveau is associated with three great and very different designers, all of whom produced work of extraordinary originality. The arabesque made a return appearance, and the Belgian Victor Horta is notable for his sinuous use of ironwork and his adaptation of Rococo delicacies. The Scot Charles Rennie Mackintosh developed the idea of the exaggerated vertical, borrowed from both Celtic and Japanese art and heralding the modernism of the Bauhaus. The Spaniard Antonio Gaudi designed an apartment block in Barcelona in the first decade of the twentieth century that contained the most fantastically inventive interiors of the pre-war era. Taking up the native Moorishness of Spanish tradition and combining it with a highly decorated Gothicism, he created rooms which banish corners, squares and rectangles for a whirling succession of convoluted curves and twisting spirals.

Acceptable Nonsense

After the First World War, romantic illusion within interior decoration was inspired largely by the theatre. A spate of exotic interiors were modelled on the stage sets of Alexandre Benois and Leon Bakst, designed for the Ballets Russes, notably the sets for *Scheherazade* and *The Sleeping Princess*. In the 1920s in England a somewhat lighter and more frolicsome style returned, epitomized in the fancy-dress balls and elegant *fêtes champêtres* of such painters and designers as Rex Whistler and Oliver Messel. Cecil Beaton decorated his house at Ashcombe in Wiltshire in this vein, once described as 'a kind of twentieth-century folly'. Simon Harcourt-Smith's sadly forgotten novel *The Last of Uptake* (1941) aptly suggests the flavour:

> The grotto was contrived in the shape of a snail's shell, with passages that spiralled inward from room to room. There was a chamber like the Snow King's audience hall, another pearly one that must have been Venus's ballroom . . . in one of the sconces, made from coral branches and shells, there was still a candle . . .

This European interior is decorated in the extremely lavish and exotic style popular from the 1850s. The peacock and various oriental artefacts, the ubiquitous palm, the heavy, fringed curtain draped across the doorway and the tiles around the fireplace all add to the opulent atmosphere.

The only way in which to describe this dressing room in a Paris apartment of the 1840s, painted by François-Etienne Villeret, is 'romantic'. One is enveloped in a luxurious sea of silk hangings, decorated with a light floral pattern and perfectly complemented by the light furniture, some of it painted. The furnishings are reminiscent of the Rococo and Louis XIV periods, typical of the eclectic taste of French interior decoration at this time.

This bedroom scheme for the London house of Miss Faye Dunaway perfectly illustrates the contemporary romantic reverie.

This mural, which might at first glance seem to date from the seventeenth century, was in fact painted in 1936 by Rex Whistler. It forms part of the scheme of wall paintings in the dining room at Plas Newydd in Anglesey, which the artist painted for Sir Philip Sassoon in the late 1930s, and which so splendidly demonstrate the timeless nature of the romantic ideal.

It was all a quixotic game for the leisured upper classes, determined to enjoy themselves in the lull after the storm of the First World War. Escape is the essence of romantic fantasy. In the middle decades of the twentieth century, escape for the majority came through the silver screen and the products of that great dream factory, Hollywood. Those cream-and-silk interiors that typify the romantic comedies of stars like Carole Lombard and Katharine Hepburn became a common decorative fantasy.

An effect of mass media, however, is to stereotype images in such a way that fantasy becomes less individual as a set repertoire of images becomes only too familiar. But there is always a place for the romantic spirit to create a truly unique environment, such as the fairy-tale Victorian house of painter Graham Ovenden in Cornwall.

Entertainment rather than need: is this perhaps the essence of romantic style today? The spirit of the fairy godmother's magic wand that transforms the ordinariness of everyday into the extraordinary. This idea is encapsulated in a comment by Laura Ashley:

> You can turn your whole living space into a leafy conservatory if you wish, or a stage set waiting for its players in fancy dress. Today, no one is going to be surprised. Nonsense is very acceptable at last.

Nowadays, interior decoration can provide the means for anyone to indulge their own romantic reveries, their own dream combinations of colours, fabrics and furnishings. Whether it is a world of pavilions, tented ceilings and chivalry or one of lace, frills and flowers, the realization of personal fantasies – Laura Ashley's 'nonsense' – is often the inspiration for today's most captivating decorative schemes.

ROMANTIC STYLE
Laura Ashley

Infusing fantasy into everyday life is the essence of the romantic. It is an invitation to indulge in extravagance and audacious effects, an opportunity to turn the inspiration of past styles, like that of the medieval pavilion, into a look which is entirely individual.

The desire for a truly romantic room, whether it exists as an evocation of the past, or of distant lands, or a particular mood, has never been more prevalent in the history of interior decoration than it is today. While Laura Ashley have long been associated with the nostalgic romanticism of Victorian England, a world filled with lace and roses, they also provide the means for everyone to realize their own fantasies, to become their own set-designer. 'Romantic style is the daydream of its creator', and as such it is perceived in many ways. It may evoke the femininity of a bedroom of palest pink, filled with a profusion of chintz roses, the theatrical opulence of the tented boudoirs of the Arabian Nights, or a cool, flower-filled retreat from the heat of a tropical sun.

For Laura Ashley, the key to such a transformation lies in the delicate combination of subtle colours, beautiful fabrics and exquisite finishing touches which together lend an air of indulgent extravagance and luxury. A Gothic bathroom is washed in ice-cream colours of pistacchio green and rose pink, while an intimate study is given dramatic allure by painting it vivid scarlet. A soft fall of muslin around a bedhead, a length of creamy white lace, fabrics across which garlands of flowers tumble and ribbons twist and turn – this is the stuff of which dreams are made, bringing romance into everyday life □

In a conservatory, the house meets the garden. This beautiful example, designed about a hundred years ago, is attached to a château in northern France. Fabrics echo the flowery profusion of the garden with posies and ribbons – a peaceful, romantic corner for a summer picnic of strawberries and cream.

A deeply romantic bedroom in a soft shade of pink, centring on a glorious bed of roses. The heady theme was a natural extension of the old rose-garden overlooked from the window. To its virtues of intimacy and melting colour have been added the flamboyance of a half-tester bed and an assertive sense of style.

Two prints on a major and minor theme are mingled throughout for an integrated, but not monotonous, look. The counterpane, bed hangings and window curtains are splashed with an extravagance of full-blown cabbage roses; the valance, inner bed hangings, sofa, stool and footstool are sprinkled with rosebuds, both prints unified by a trellis background. Cushions are in a haphazard mixture of both. In this way, roses luxuriate over everything without becoming overbearing.

Romanticism is balanced by walls washed shell pink – light, plain and roseless except for a garlanded border which is just enough to carry the mood through. Not everything is pink, however. The velvet stool at the foot of the bed and a predominantly blue rug are counterpoints. The key to this sort of room is knowing how much of any one element is enough.

Controlled frills and flounces ruffle cushions, hangings and the edge of the curtains. Pictures pick out deeper spots of pink, and a beribboned escritoire has the same capricious feel. A magnificent arrangement of peonies and Madonna lilies heightens the flowery effect.

A bedroom and bathroom in a West Country house created the opportunity for a continuous decorative scheme to link two rooms. White and sapphire blue are the unifying colours, the bedroom further freshened by a cowslip yellow. The links between the two rooms are subtle as each has a different mood. The bedroom has the ethereal romanticism of gently draped muslin, while the bathroom, though imbued with the same softness at the window, has an all-over crispness with strong stripes on the window seat.

The bedroom is up-in-the-clouds, with its summer-sky ceiling reflected in the colour-washed lower walls. A delicate chandelier, its wrought iron loops like a fine necklace, is a French copy of a seventeenth-century original. The wrought iron bedstead has the same fine line, and it is in such lightness that the innocence of the room lies: the wickerwork Lloyd loom chair, a bare floor and featherlight muslin, draped over the mantel and above all, the bedhead. An arched recess provides a perfect frame for its diaphanous swathes.

The same muslin is festooned gauzily over the bathroom window to soften its lines and echo the mood of the bedroom. A sprig and trellis print under the washbasin and on a comfortable armchair have the same feminine influence. Blue and white wallpaper is hung in both rooms, but only above dado level to give the same sense of proportion in each.

What could be more romantic than a Victorian morning room bathed in early light, its French windows giving onto the garden and inviting a walk upon the dewy grass after breakfast? The themes of garden and morning sunshine are the natural ones to adopt inside. The whole room is gilded with cowslip yellow – in simple stripes on the wallpaper, in glorious golden roses on the chintz framing the window and covering the sofa. The window is given the special treatment it deserves, with a full, softly gathered pelmet and curtains that just brush the floor, their fullness caught by matching tie-backs. The roses are carried through at cornice level with a garlanded border in fresh contrast to the subtle stripes of the paper. Even the carpet is yellow in tone. A verdant fringed tablecloth has a subtle golden trim, and a quaint Victorian spoonback chair and stool add to the complexity of texture and tone. The pair of rugs are particularly beautiful, with a profusion of faded garden blooms winding over them in arabesques, as though the garden had continued underfoot into the room.

A straightforward wooden chair is drawn into the overall ambience with a padded, fitted and frilled cover in lightly sketched checks. The top of a corner cupboard, an often neglected space, is brought to life by two laurel-leaved lovers, which add to the gently stressed romanticism of the room.

This tented boudoir is the epitome of an unrestrained romanticism of the most opulent and exotic kind. The room has been created from that small, uninteresting space often found on the half landing of London houses. It has unsymmetrical alcoves which have been effectively disguised by these sumptuous drapes. A romantic style such as this delights in trompe l'oeil and sleight of hand.

The swagged pelmet is based on one of the earliest recorded designs for a tented room in England (1800). The effect of a *tour de force* is aimed for and achieved by covering everything with one pattern: crimson stripes on a sumptuous yellow ground, scattered with sprays of flowers. It was based on a fragment of eighteenth-century hand-painted silk in the Whitworth Museum, Manchester. The crimson of the roses in the cloth is emphasized by a specially dyed linen fringe and the cushions, two of which are seventeenth-century Spanish silk with old gold Moorish appliqués. The jewel-like nature of the room, with its ottoman for lounging beneath the window, gives it an Oriental flavour, the East being a recurrent theme in romantic design. A pierced Egyptian brass stand adds a note of enigma, and the gilded copper lamp is eighteenth-century Venetian. The acanthus leaf tie-backs are Victorian, and the little writing desk is another curiosity with four candle stands that swing out at the corners and remain tantalizingly level no matter how far the table top is twisted and turned.

The Gothic strain in romantic style has been combined with the more familiar flowery abundance to create this luxurious and unusual bathroom. It starts with every advantage, however, by being unusually spacious with a splendid bay window. This is played up to the full, with window seats all round. Frilled, rowan-sprigged curtains are piped with rose pink for added definition and caparisoned with Regency rosettes and bows. Full-length cloths in the same fabric are flung over tables to provide a setting for personal mementos: silver-framed photographs, antique scent bottles with silver stoppers, mirrors, powder boxes.

The Victorian Gothic mood is established in the dominant colour of soft jade green, and characterized by the stylized 'Gothic' arches which give so much interest to the room. These are picked out in a paler shade (white satin gloss mixed with jade), as are cornice, and bath and washbasin panelling. The washbasin alcove has a wonderfully ostentatious mirror with two brackets on either side mimicking traditional sconces, but in fact bearing after-shave and scent. The lavatory closet is arrayed with shell-encrusted pictures and frames, a faint reminder of the grotto-esque. Other 'Gothic' elements to the room are the heavy X-frame stool, and such associations of bygone richness as the tapestry-covered screen. The arches are framed by bow-tied lengths of the rowan-sprigged cotton to unify the two themes.

An inspired idea for transforming a
simple bed into an enchanting bower.
In a small room like this, a four-poster
would be overwhelming; this corner
bed, taken from a nineteenth-century
watercolour by Marcel Blairat, has the
same poetic effect with a more
economical use of space. The chintz is
a concoction of deep pink sweet peas
with jade tendrils twined between,
echoing the texture-patterned sea-
green wallpaper. Bed curtains and
counterpane are all in chintz; the
deeply-frilled valance and the pelmet
with a design of rosettes and softly
inverted pleats was taken from a mid-
nineteenth century upholsterer's
guide. The curtains are pulled back to
swag romantically round the bed. The
darker pink picked out on the sweet
peas is subtly continued in the
wallpaper border of trompe l'oeil
twisted braid.

The rest of the room is peaceful and
pretty. Sweet peas are scattered on
frilled and piped cushions alike,
softening the hard edges of furniture.
The dressing table is swathed in
chintz (which here takes a little border
of lace) and arrayed with Victorian
accessories and a Regency burr walnut
toilet mirror with drawers for powder
puffs and trinkets. All the furniture,
apart from a mahogany armchair, is
beech, painted with original Victorian
designs. A washstand with jug and
basin makes a charming addition,
above which hangs an exquisite piece
of unfinished embroidery on ivory
satin, begun in about 1700.

The term 'romantic' does not always mean flowers and need not necessarily mean feminine. It can also mean the extravagance of taking an idea to its limit, as in this scarlet study. The result is a luxurious enclave, which provides a retreat from a mundane world. Two very ordinary materials have been used to extraordinary effect: paint and chintz. The key is the lavishness with which they have been applied – everything, but everything, is scarlet. It is unusual enough to have bright red walls, but here the panelling has been washed in scarlet as well. The boldest stroke, however, was painting the fireplace bold red to contrast with the black hearth and echo the real flames within it.

The intensity of a single effect, repeatedly used, comes into play with fabric as well. Chintz has been used for sofa, library chair, pleated lampshades, tablecloths, and even for the plump cushion in the dog basket. This is a room which comes into its own in the evening when the lustre of chintz can be played up to the hilt with candles and soft lights, creating a dramatic chiaroscuro. Contrasting deep shadow is essential to the effect, and brings a richness to the red tones. Shadows are cleverly enhanced by heavier fabrics in dark crimsons which absorb the light: a kelim on the red carpet, antique gold and crimson cushions on the sofa, the swagged curtains, dark velvet-upholstered stools and, above all, the soft heavy folds of the table carpet on the desk. The sumptuous sense of texture is enhanced by a very generous, red-dyed bullion fringe on sofa, table carpet and curtains.

This Florida verandah is a tropical haven from the heat of the midday sun, an arbour of shade and cool.

The mood is set by the colours of the room – whitewashed walls, unpainted wooden trellises, the terracotta of tubs and floor tiles, the honey tones of cane and rattan furniture, and against this the bombastic pink of a glorious excess of hydrangeas. The main fabric used picks up these colours, its muted white stripes on a sand ground providing a link between the warmer tones of the furniture and the whitewashed walls. Some of the cushions are self-piped and others are piped in white to underpin this. The mulberry-coloured sprig matches the hydrangeas. Where large areas of cloth are needed, such as for the huge Roman blind that fills one arch, and the ottoman below it, this print is used. A richer flower print is needed, however, to take the eye comfortably from the tiny sprig to the huge heads of the hydrangeas. This is provided by a lyrical print of wild flowers in dark pink and blue on a spice-coloured ground that draws the colours of trellis and floor tiles into the room. It is used more sparingly and given a burgundy piping.

Full use is made of the room's height with glossy-leaved trees in big terracotta tubs and troughs. The trellis is an important key to the cool mood. It is fretted to give a Moorish feel and casts patterns of light and shade on the tiles, further filtered by the jungle of leaves outside. An old-fashioned wooden fan stirs the air with just the right sound of gentle whirring to accompany a siesta.

The naturally romantic setting of this French château required a reflective, lyrical treatment in sympathy with its surroundings. This is the ante-room, a formal 'informal' room where drinks are taken before lunch or dinner; and it is also used as the family sitting room when the drawing room would be too grand. Its great assets are the multitude of windows, which permit a soft afternoon light to filter through, and the balustraded stone terrace beyond, which leads onto the garden. A pier glass reflects the set of windows opposite to add to the airy spaciousness of the room. Such a focal point required curtains in a print both confident enough to harmonize with the grand scheme of the room and informal enough to provide a relaxing background. This wandering floral design of gracefully windblown roses and fuschias on an understated sand-coloured background proved ideal. The curtains are held casually by matching tie-backs, and decorated with more formal, fringed pelmets above to give these magnificent windows the grand frame they deserve.

The armchairs are covered in a more closely-flowered cotton, appropriate to their smaller size, and a stylized sprig is used on the sofa with a faded wickerwork pattern in sand and white on cushions and tablecloths. This clever mixing of patterns instantly brings an air of relaxation to the room. The overall result is a wistfully beautiful room, sensitive to the picturesque countryside beyond, with an atmosphere of gracious ease.

PERIOD

STYLE

PERIOD STYLE
Past Traditions

Everyone has an image of a 'period' house, whether it be Georgian (like this exterior view painted by John S. Goodall), Victorian, or taken from the 1920s. Most of us have some idea of another age at which it might have been interesting to have lived, and increasingly people are attempting to restore their houses to their original appearance.

Since the architects and philosophers of the Italian Renaissance first looked back to the ancient world for inspiration, designers – both professional and amateur – have been obsessed with reproducing the styles of past eras. For the eighteenth century, it was the gleaming marble splendours of the classical world that dominated the European imagination. The nineteenth century followed with a variety of stylistic revivals. A delight in the medieval was kindled by the enormously popular *Waverley* novels of Walter Scott, the first to take times gone by as their subject and paint them with rich, vivid details of ancient customs, speech, clothes and furnishings.

Today, with the aid of numerous works on the stylistic details and techniques of every past period, from ancient Egypt to the Europe of the 1930s, it is possible to transport a room back in time to the era of your choice. Yet the successful restoration of a period interior, or even the creation of a past style in a home with a more modern pedigree, relies not only on historical authenticity. The secret lies in understanding the spirit of the time, the lifestyles of that particular era, how the rooms were used, the private and public faces of the home. In this way the decorative styles of the past – whether Georgian, Regency, Victorian or thirties' style – can be brought to life again with all the comforts of the twentieth century ☐

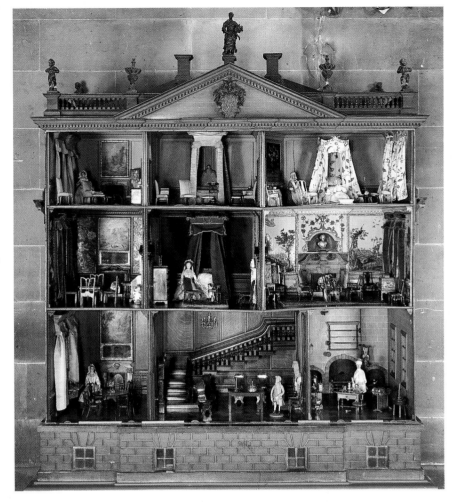

The unique Chippendale doll's house at Nostell Priory in Yorkshire provides a perfect re-creation in miniature of a house of the 1740s. The entrance hall is panelled in oak, with a parquet floor, while an open fire in the marble fireplace is tended by a liveried footman. To the left of the hall, the daughter of the house busies herself in the parlour, where a Dutch-influenced landscape hangs on the panelled walls above a black-leaded grate. To the right of the hall another footman is polishing the silver in the kitchen. On the first floor the master bedroom is decorated with elaborate red velvet hangings; to the left, the dressing room has a chimneypiece of black marble and walls painted in the Chinese style; on the right, the formal drawing room is elaborately decorated in yellow and gold, with painted panels depicting scenes of pastoral life. On the top floor, the bedroom and dressing room are decorated with yellow silk hangings, suggesting that they belong to the lady of the house; to the right, a child's room is hung with an Indian floral chintz which is perfectly complemented by the mid blue of the painted walls.

The visual re-creation of the past is one of the addictions of modern Western society. It begins with the acquisition of a period home, one built in the 1740s perhaps. You may be lucky enough to find a Rococo-style table in keeping with the style of the house, and before you know it the entire interior has come to resemble a stage set for *The Marriage of Figaro*. Osbert Lancaster summed up the Victorian equivalent succinctly in *Here Of All Places* (1959):

> The second avenue of escape from . . . austerity led, not to the jungles of the Amazon, but straight back to great aunt Harriet's front parlour . . . In due course one Victorian work-table almost inevitably heralded the arrival of a whole summer of ottomans, Aubussons, beadwork firescreens, Martin engravings, lustres . . .

Period furnishings can be used in very different ways: furnishings from one period can be used with those of another to create a comfortable eclecticism; they can become an elegant veneer when used alongside conventional modern technology; or period detail can be applied either to a house of a particular period or to a modern purpose-built apartment, transforming both into a decorative time capsule.

In the nineteenth century the first approach was widely favoured, producing the characteristic 'eclectic confusion' of the Victorian interior. The second can be seen in the work of A. W. N. Pugin, to whose work the 'pointed Christian' architecture and decoration of the mid-Victorian Gothic revival lent a veneer of high moral significance. The third approach was also taken up during the nineteenth century, as can be seen in this account of a visit to Cothele in Cornwall in 1827, from *The Three Howard Sisters* by Lady Leconfield and John Gore:

> We found an excellent dinner prepared in that delightful dining room you must remember. One really felt transported to the time in which the house was built; everything in such perfect keeping and character, the old pewter plates, with family arms, the tall, narrow wine glasses, the salt cellars, spoons, forks, tankards and salvers etc. all in complete unison.

The passion for period authenticity gradually came to affect designers throughout Europe, although Britain led the way. In the 1920s there was a resurgence in England of interest in the Georgian style of decoration, following the publication of such works as Ramsay's *Small Houses of the Georgian Period*, and *English Interiors in Smaller Houses* by Margaret Jourdain. In the 1930s, as the modern movement lost favour among the upper classes, more people began to look back in time for inspiration. A new enthusiasm for period detail among architects, particularly such classicists as Raymond Erith and Lord Gerald Wellesley, quickly spread to the world of interior decoration.

Period style is designed to deceive. To see the transformation in action, let us try to uncover four such re-creations: a Georgian town house of the 1730s; a Regency town house of 1815; a Victorian house of the 1860s; and an avant-garde interior of the 1920s.

A Georgian Town House of the 1730s

Life in England in the 1730s was a difficult one. In 1727 George II had succeeded his father as king. In the world of art, William Hogarth satirized society and captured the atmosphere of London's streets and fashionable interiors. But it was not a healthy society in which to live: three in four children died before the age of six, and the average life expectancy was thirty-five years. Poor health was not confined to the needy: fevers and poxes were commonplace, while typhus and influenza often rose to epidemic proportions. If paupers suffered from scurvy, the rich groaned from gout, and ladies were even known to have died from the excessive lead content in their heavily applied cosmetics.

ABOVE A Tea Party at Lord Harrington's House, *painted by Charles Philips in 1730, evokes the Georgian interior and lifestyle. A tea-drinking 'assembly' is in progress, the blue and white tea service possibly imported from China, and a game of cards continues in the other corner. The panelled walls are painted in a rich blue-green tone with a matching damask wall hanging to the right.*

RIGHT *London in the eighteenth century was a rough and ready world in which to live. Covent Garden, pictured here, was particularly notorious as a centre of crime and vice. There was no proper sanitation, and the dreadful condition of the streets contrasted plainly with the fine houses.*

While the poor lived off a diet of bread, cheese and fat bacon, supplemented by tea, beer and gin, the upper classes feasted on roast beef, game, sugar, fruits and chocolate. Brandy was the most usual form of alcohol, with wine being served by the pint. Meals assumed a very different pattern from that of today: breakfast was at 10 a.m., followed by a snack at midday. There was no formal lunch, but dinner was taken in the middle of the afternoon, and the fashionable sometimes indulged in a light supper at 9 or 10 p.m. Dinner parties were frequent, often accompanied by dancing and card playing. There was also the 'assembly', a sociable evening of tea drinking and gossip. Masquerades, balls and musical parties completed the social scene. Gambling was rife, both at the gaming table and on the racetrack.

London in 1730 would have been full of the noise of the street: the cries of fishmongers, flowergirls, bakers, knife grinders, sweeps and milkmaids. Crime was rising, and the exterior of a house was designed to face up to this tough world with a solid front door reached by a bridge across a basement yard, the whole secluded behind spiked railings. London houses were built of thick brick and stucco by decree after the Great Fire of 1666.

The eighteenth century saw a great increase in speculative building – in 1720 Grosvenor Square was laid out with terraced houses in the form of Palladian mansions, producing the exterior sweep of a single palace façade with a central pediment. Inside these grand looking houses, however, the rooms were surprisingly small, usually between twelve and fifteen feet square and plainly decorated. The walls would have been panelled in pine or cedar wood above an oak wainscot. The main feature of the room would have been the chimneypiece; the chimney breast, sandwiched between two shelved recesses, would have been decorated with sculpted stucco detail, or a picture, and the fireplace beneath would have held a grate for coal in the winter and a painted chimneyboard in the summer.

The panelling would have been painted in one of a limited range of colours, although in general colours tended to become lighter as the century progressed. In the 1730s crimson and dark green were considered most appropriate for the display of paintings and for all ceremonial rooms. An alternative was a strong blue, often combined with gold; yellow was not widely favoured, and white was generally only used in the saloon. Paint effects, like graining and marbling, enhanced the surface of plain walls, and as all furniture during this period was pushed back against the walls when not in use, a dado rail was always fixed to the walls to prevent chairs from scuffing the painted panelling.

Elegant sash windows, made up of a number of small panes, were typical of the period. Floors were made of polished or painted wooden planks, or parquet. Sometimes they were blacked with soot and small

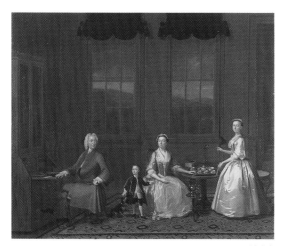

Elegant sash windows were an important feature of the Georgian town house, and would have been dressed with reefed curtains, as shown in this view of an English drawing room with its splendid patterned carpet and glazed bookcase.

In this painting by Hogarth, The Graham Children, *of 1742, we can see many of the features of the eighteenth-century house which would have seemed commonplace to its inhabitants. The floor is tiled in a contrasting chequered pattern and a heavy velvet curtain hangs to the right. The chair covering is attached in typical Georgian fashion with gilt pins, while the ornate clock appears to be an early variant of Rococo style.*

beer to disguise the dirt, and were swept night and morning with a mixture of lavender and tea which was then left next to the skirting. The boards would have been covered with a variety of Oriental and European carpets, those from the Savonnerie factory in Paris being considered particularly fine (carpets were not fitted until the 1750s). More common was the floor cloth, a piece of canvas painted a plain colour and patterned with diamonds, squares or, occasionally, a more elaborate design. Furniture was heavy and elaborately carved, and carbriole legs were to be seen in profusion, particularly with ball and claw feet. Walnut wood was the height of fashion, although a great deal of oak and beech was still in use.

In 1727 William Kent began to achieve some degree of success with his furniture designs which incorporated motifs of *putti*, swags, acanthus leaves and shells taken from Italian pieces of the sixteenth and seventeenth centuries; lacquered or 'japanned' furniture in red or black was also in favour. The most common form of table in use was the gate-leg type, and there were many kinds of cupboard for a variety of purposes – glazed corner cabinets for china, and architecturally-detailed bookcases for leather-bound volumes.

Comfortable upholstery was in its infancy. A typical armchair would have been equipped with only a squab cushion for comfort. All upholstery was secured with gilt nails and trimmed with silk or braid. Materials for chairs were as rich as possible – damasks, chintzes and velvets, with fine gold, silver, lace and galloon trims. Often separate loose covers were made up in a cheap gingham check or striped cotton to protect the finery beneath, and these would be used on all but ceremonial occasions. Motifs common on upholstery fabrics included flowers, landscapes, figures and oriental patterns.

Other accessories commonly seen in a house of this time would have been a harpsichord or spinnet, and a number of screens: fire screens to protect faces from the heat, and larger folding screens to keep out the draughts. The latter would have been papered or painted and trimmed in braid; material or Spanish leather were also used. Mirrors were commonplace; in the drawing room large mirrors were fitted into the panelling, made up from small panes within a wooden frame similar to that of the windows. In bedrooms small 'dressing mirrors' stood on the dressing table.

The porcelain of the 1730s was all imported and of oriental design, the tea cups having no handles. Houses were filled with small china ornaments: blue and white glazed earthenware from Delft and figurines of shepherds and shepherdesses from Meissen. The finest silverware was produced in England by the Huguenot silversmiths who had fled to London from religious persecution in France at the turn of the century; and the most exquisite glass available had twisted and coloured stems and splayed bowls.

Candles were the sole source of illumination in the 1730s. Made from a poorly burning wax, they were placed about the house in candlesticks, sconces, torchères and chandeliers, where they gave out a little more light with the aid of reflective cut-glass lustre drops. They could be an expensive form of lighting: the number of candles at a dinner party was taken as an indication of social status. In 1731 Horace Walpole, receiving a State visit from the French emissary, spent £15 a night lighting his hall with one hundred and thirty candles. Candles were not always white: in the 1730s the Duke of Chandos is said to have preferred candles in a lime green wax, and sometimes scented candles were used to disguise everyday aromas – myrtle was a popular and delicate fragrance.

In the wake of improvements in colour printing, wallpaper became increasingly popular as an alternative to fabric in the 1730s. It was generally of flock (a new invention in imitation of velvet), damask, silk or needlework, and was hung only to wainscot level. Typical motifs were birds, plants or figures, but from the late 1720s, imported Chinese papers also appeared, printed with designs of flora and fauna.

The most elaborately decorated room in the house was the drawing room, with its cornicing, chimneypiece and carpets, stout oak doors, and windows with elaborately carved mouldings. Each window would have had a pair of full shutters as well as a single curtain reefed up into a festoon. The main bedroom would have had panelling hung to dado level with velvet or tapestry in winter, silk or satin in summer, with curtains in the same fabric or motif. Apart from the heavy drapery surrounding the four-poster bed, vital for the exclusion of pervasive draughts, the furniture would have been scanty. The kitchen would have been bleak, with walls plastered in plain blue or green – colours supposed to discourage flies. The stone floor would have been covered with straw and most of the food would still have been cooked on a spit over an open fire.

A Regency Town House of 1815

By 1815, Georgian Britain was a very different place, transformed by the effects of the early Industrial Revolution and twenty years of war in Europe against Napoleon. In 1811 George III had been declared insane, and his spendthrift son – crowned George IV in 1820 – had taken formal monarchical powers with the title of Prince Regent. The period of the Regency was one in which the extravagant taste of the future king influenced everything from morals and manners to fashionable vogues. The vanity and upper-class excess of the time was embodied in the rise of the Dandy, a man whose only commitment was his own pleasure: Beau Brummel was his model, the Prince Regent his dubious hero.

TOP *In the eighteenth century lighting was all important, and indeed social functions were often adjudged by the degree of candlelight provided by the host. This masquerade at the King's Opera House in the Haymarket, London, was obviously a very grand affair, with candelabra and chandeliers hanging from the ceiling and lining the walls – it is reported that some 500 wax lights were used.*

ABOVE *This sporting screen was painted in the mid eighteenth century for an Irish magistrate and keen supporter of all forms of horsemanship. Twelve hunting scenes are charmingly rendered by the painter Richard Roper.*

LEFT *This room in a French house of the post-Empire period is typical of the increased informality which pervaded interior decoration during the Regency era. The entire room has been covered with a simple blue-striped wallpaper to create a tent-like effect, without the exoticism commonly associated with such schemes. The curtains use the same fabric, and the fringing on the shaped pelmet echoes the skirting border.*

During the period, and particularly among the upper and middle classes, a sense of lightness and frivolity prevailed. Disease was no longer of the epidemic proportions that had characterized the Georgian era, and there was a drastic drop in the number of infant deaths. The values of family and home became increasingly important, although as one can see from the behaviour of the Musgrove family in Jane Austen's novel *Persuasion* (1818), social attitudes were becoming more relaxed. Life became more entertaining for women; liberated from wigs and constricting corsets, they were now able to relax in simple but sophisticated clothes made from light cottons and muslin.

New houses were frequently constructed of Portland stone rather than brick; sometimes they were faced with stucco and painted to resemble stone. The internal plan did not differ greatly from that of the earlier Georgian town house with two rooms on each storey, but interiors were much lighter, more colourful and better maintained.

Larger windows made the rooms brighter. They were still of the sash variety, but now had narrower glazing bars and fewer, larger panes, usually only six, and in the drawing room they often extended to floor level. All windows were fitted with full-length internal shutters, and were often decorated with elaborate tied-back draperies, hung from a pole. These were of silk, linen or chintz, often striped or otherwise printed with small sprigged floral designs of the kind that was fashionable for dress fabrics at the time.

BELOW *During the Regency period the exterior design of houses changed to reflect the more casual lifestyle. Greater use was made of Portland stone, or local stone, as seen here in Bath, and more emphasis was placed on natural light as sash windows increased in size.*

Wallpapers became increasingly popular, their vivid colours generally chosen to echo the colour and design of the upholstery and draperies. Papers were often striped, sometimes in satin or flock, while some were printed in a clever imitation of marble. Favourite designs were yellow and black stripes, and an abstract spot pattern, printed in blue and black.

The chimneypiece, too, was given a lighter touch, being made from white marble with gilt or contrasting marble decoration. Beneath a shallow mantelpiece the fireplace would have contained a hob grate on paw feet, possibly with a pair of elaborate Egyptian-style fire-dogs.

Floors were still of polished wood and spread with rugs or carpets, but these were now mostly of English manufacture – Axminster, Kidderminster or Wilton – with a central floral pattern and co-ordinating border.

Furniture was no longer formally arranged and pushed back against the wall when not in use, but elegantly grouped at varying angles in order to make conversation easier and more intimate. The decoration and furniture of the period was much influenced by the ideas of Thomas Hope, a rich tradesman and amateur designer with a penchant for ancient and Far Eastern civilizations, which he had visited on his many travels, collecting various treasures along the way. Hope deplored the 'degraded' influence of the French Rococo and advocated something much more striking and masculine. He mixed strong colours on walls, floors and furniture: the 'Indian' room of his own house sported sky-blue walls, a pale yellow ceiling, crimson upholstery and decorative details in azure and sea green. Although this was a ceremonial room, knowledge of its design reached the public through Hope's *Household Furniture and Interior Decoration* (1807), and had a considerable influence on the fashionable interior.

Regency furniture, many parts of which were now machine-made, was influenced by Hope's ideas and became characterized by a great deal of painting and gilding. Favoured woods were satinwood veneer, rosewood and mahogany. The most comfortable chairs and sofas had a cane base, painted wooden frame and squab cushions in bright fabrics. A popular piece of the period was the 'Grecian couch', a classical design usually made in mahogany or rosewood with serpentine back and sides, claw and ball feet and round bolster cushions. A Greek key motif might have patterned the upholstery of silk, damask, brocade, chintz or plain cotton. Other typical items of Regency furniture included sofa tables with fold-up leaves; large, heavy sideboards; unglazed bookcases; and neat writing cabinets and escritoires.

Owing to improved methods of production, panes of glass had become larger and mirrors – often convex and circular, in carved or gilded frames topped by an eagle or floral design – were employed to great

This pair of watercolours by Humphry Repton shows quite clearly the enormous changes which took place in interior design during the early years of the nineteenth century. Above, we can see the typical Georgian interior: a small, somewhat cramped room lit from two high, narrow windows and with little furniture, save a few formally arranged chairs which occupy the central space of the room. Below is the new Regency ideal: a light and airy conservatory lit by larger windows and opening onto the garden through French doors. The chairs are now grouped around the walls, allowing people to pursue their individual pastimes, or to converse freely, as they so wished.

illusionistic effect. Longcase clocks, now out of fashion, were replaced by chic pendulum and shelf clocks, ornately decorated with allegorical figures.

Porcelain was more colourfully glazed and lavishly gilded than before; Minton, Spode and Wedgwood were popular manufacturers. Cut flowers began to make their way on to the drawing room tables. Glassware was more delicate, cut in shallow relief, while silver designs achieved an austerity of line and ornament which were unmatched for over a century to come.

Lighting was still a matter of candles held in chandeliers, torchères, sconces or candlesticks, on special occasions being surrounded by wreaths of flowers. A primitive oil lamp, the Argand, had been invented, but its fumes made rooms extremely dirty and prevented it from becoming widely used. Heating still relied on the open fire and, given the larger size of room without any corresponding improvement in insulation, was often ineffective. A certain Lady Elizabeth Grosvenor at Eaton Hall, Cheshire, is said to have been permanently clad in flannel underwear, two pairs of stockings and wrist mufflers!

A Victorian Interior of the 1860s

By 1860, Queen Victoria had been on the throne for twenty-three years and Lord Palmerston was the Prime Minister of a strong Whig government. Britain was unique in the degree of liberty it permitted, but the living conditions for the industrial poor were appalling, as the novels of Dickens revealed. Yet Victorian culture was varied and thriving. At the forefront of artistic circles was the Pre-Raphaelite Brotherhood, while Ruskin and Morris advocated good craftsmanship and ornament as an alternative to the dreariness of the factory-made. Photography began to make its mark too. In intellectual life, Charles Darwin's *The Origin of Species* shocked society by proclaiming man's descent from the apes; George Eliot's *Adam Bede*, a compassionate novel of country life, and Tennyson's Arthurian epic poem *Idylls of the King* provided more relaxing reading.

Despite technological improvements like the sewing machine, domestic life for the servant class was still a daily drudgery. An entry in the extraordinary diary of Hannah Cullwick for 14 July 1860 records an existence little better than slavery:

> Wash'd up in the scullery. Clean'd the pantry on my knees & scour'd the tables. Scrubbed the flags around the house & clean'd the window sills. Got tea at 9 for the master & Mrs Warwick in my

LEFT *Queen Victoria and Prince Albert, pictured in their private railway carriage. A fitting image to convey the Victorian ideal of a well-furnished room. The chairs are heavily upholstered, as are the walls, while at the window hang curtains of an unprecedented weight, decked with an assortment of superfluous tassels and swags. On the floor is a patterned 'wall to wall' carpet.*

BELOW *A typical mid-Victorian interior. The walls are covered with a densely patterned fabric and hung with nostalgic landscapes. Above the fireplace stands a huge chimneypiece with a pair of glittering glass lustres and an assortment of curios under their ubiquitous glass domes.*

dirt, but Ann carried it up. Clean'd the privy & passage & scullery floor on my knees. Wash'd the dog & clean'd the sinks down. Put the supper ready for Ann to take up, for I was too dirty & tired to go upstairs ...

Houses had become much taller since the Regency period, incorporating extra rooms on the attic floors for wretched servants like Hannah. The brick and stone façade was characterized by the new bay window; interiors were still relatively restrained for the eclectic confusion and clutter we associate with the Victorian age had not yet taken hold.

Paper was by now the usual means of decorating a wall; dark tones of crimson, blue and green, with a strong pattern of fauna and flora motifs were most popular. The surrounding paintwork would have been dark brown, the ceiling plain white. The dado rail was less in evidence, now replaced by a tall frieze above and a dado area below, papered or stencilled in a different pattern to that of the wallpaper. Below the frieze might be a picture rail and at the foot of the wall a four-foot dado area and one-foot wainscot. The focal point of the major rooms was still the chimneypiece, made from marble, cast iron or wood, and elaborately decorated with floral designs and a series of shelves and mirrors.

The sash windows had larger panes than ever before, while the doors were of four panels and often covered with a velvet curtain on a brass pole. The shuttered windows were draped with curtains of thick velvet or damask, hung from mahogany or brass poles, often with a lace curtain underneath; decorative roller blinds were now a common form of window dressing as well.

The oak floors of such a house would have fitted carpets of complex patterns in deep colours. Brussels weave carpet was believed to be the best, but Kidderminster was almost as good, a hard-wearing carpet with a deep pile. Decorated floor cloths, made from heavy Scottish canvas and coated with four layers of thick paint, were still in use.

Furniture was in general heavier than before. The most fashionable wood was mahogany, and the styles were based on the Rococo or Gothic, both with a great deal of decoration. Typical were the wing armchair, the button-back chair with an upholstered seat, and the basketwork seat with a squab cushion. Upholstery was itself much more comfortable, incorporating the new spiral spring. Fashionable covers were dark crimson and dark green, in velvet, damask or needlework, as well as the ubiquitous cabbage rose design in silk. Tables were of mahogany, oak or papier mâché, with work tables in rosewood or walnut. There was a profusion of smaller pieces of furniture – canterburies, hall stands, whatnots, cupboards and dressers – each with a specific function. In the dining room one would invariably find a solid sideboard, often of Rococo inspiration, in mahogany.

This was the era of the piano as the indispensable feature of the house, the chief source of family entertainment. Candles were no longer the main source of light, since gas was now common and effective: however, it was rarely used on the upper floors, where oil lamps and candles still prevailed. The open fire was still the only form of heating, but coal was now of better quality and fires were kept burning throughout the day. (Hannah Cullwick had a kitchen fire burning in high summer!)

Porcelain, like everything else of the period, had become extremely ornate, and glassware was heavier with deeper engraving. The desire to display collections of objects, curios and mementos grew as the century advanced: in 1860 such displays were still confined to traditional areas, perhaps with the additions of some artificial and pressed flowers or wax mouldings under glass domes.

The mid-Victorian interior was in general a dark and oppressive place, reflecting the moral and emotional tenor of the time. Solidity and durability were valued; fun and spontaneity were not.

Drawing rooms were characteristically very dark and often contained a large circular table covered in a needlework or tapestry tablecloth. On the walls hung paintings or prints by the leading artists of the day: Ford Madox Brown, Millais, Arthur Hughes, Holman Hunt, Rossetti, William Dyce, Frith and others. Alongside these hung prints of statesmen and reproduction old masters. There might also have been a few family photographs in sepia.

The bedroom would have been altogether lighter in atmosphere than the drawing room, with softer, brighter decoration and less clutter, curtains of chintz, and woodwork and built-in cupboards painted plain

This room in New York dates from the 1860s and show the eclecticism of Victorian taste, whether in Britain or the United States, with its 'Elizabethan' armchair, a Regency work table and a pair of pedestals in the Louis XV style. In a room of Gothic proportions, with a correspondingly coffered ceiling, the arched window overlooking the River Hudson is hung with lace drapery.

This portrait of the Hatch family was painted by Eastman Johnson, the most accomplished practitioner of the informal, domestic 'portrait interior' in America during the 1870s. It demonstrates the conventional sobriety of the Victorian interior. The family are gathered around a central mahogany table, the children in their rightful place are playing quietly, the father is dutifully working at his desk. Their contentment is demonstrative of the spirit of the age, as are the modest lace curtains behind the heavier drapes, the advanced gas lamp suspended from the ceiling and the ornately patterned carpet which covers the floor.

white. The furniture would have consisted of a large bed, possibly a fourposter, a muslin-draped dressing table, a wardrobe, bedside table, chair, washstand, and several mirrors. It was fashionable for the decoration of the curtains to match that of the bed drapes, which were fewer and lighter, in keeping with current medical views on health.

An Avant-garde Interior of the 1920s

The Britain of the 1920s had lost much of its imperial confidence and its Victorian pieties. Nothing could be the same after the devastations of the First World War, and society resolutely turned its face from a heritage that could have led to such a catastrophe. Victorian stuffiness was decisively rejected and there was a widespread feeling that European civilization had to start again and afresh. Writers and artists looked to the machine to provide a new aesthetic principle: radical experiments with language and visual representation followed on each other's heels, associated with such names as James Joyce, Virginia Woolf, Pablo Picasso and Vassily Kandinsky. Clothes, popular music and interior decoration loosened and brightened up too, and the pre-war decadence of Oscar Wilde, the Symbolists and Art Nouveau gave way to a spirit that was much more hopeful, positive and energetic.

At the centre of the attempt to escape from the restrictions and repressions of pre-war culture was the Bloomsbury Group, a collection of London-based intellectuals led by Virginia Woolf, the economist Maynard Keynes, the painter Duncan Grant, the art historian Roger Fry, and the writer Lytton Strachey. In their personal lives and in their various spheres, they stood for boldness, freedom and experimentation.

These characteristics are embodied in the Sussex farmhouse which Duncan Grant and Vanessa Bell took as a holiday house in 1916 and kept for the rest of their lives – Charleston, near Lewes. In 1913, along with Roger Fry and others of the set, Bell and Grant had founded the Omega Workshops, the aim of which was to produce fabrics, ceramics and furniture in a style strongly influenced by the principles of Post Impressionism. Their success had been limited and the enterprise folded in 1919, but many of the best Omega ideas found their way to Charleston, a rambling eighteenth-century building, nestling in downland, 'very solid and simple, with flat walls in that lovely mixture of brick and flint that they use about here and perfectly flat windows in the walls and wonderfully tiled roofs … the rooms are very large and a great many,' wrote Vanessa Bell to Roger Fry.

The most striking feature of the Charleston interior is the profusion of painted decoration, sometimes deliberately naïve and giving the impression of improvisation, but always exuberant, inventive and

At the height of the Victorian era one universally popular feature of interior design was the use of polychromatic schemes on ceilings, walls and furniture. In contrast to earlier treatments, colours were now deep and dark – brick-red, brown and black being the staples, picked out with small brighter areas of green, powder blue and pink. This design, which takes the inspiration for its ornament from Italianate motifs, was executed on a ceiling.

This Music Room, designed by Duncan Grant and Vanessa Bell in the 1930s, includes many characteristic features of the Bloomsbury style. The designs are all loosely painted in an almost amateur way, derived from the Cubist preoccupation with primitive art which had already manifested itself at the Omega Workshops under the direction of Roger Fry. The decorative picture of a still life is painted directly onto the wall and given a trompe l'oeil drapery frame. Beneath it stands a painted cabinet and beside this a chair, fitted with a loose cover to match that of the sofa and the curtains. The colours are muted shades of yellow and purple, typical of the exuberant Bloomsbury designers.

witty. The art historian Richard Morphet has described the overall effect as ranging from 'formal boldness to humorous intimacy. It embraces walls, doors, panelling, fire surrounds, fabrics, chairs, tables, cupboards, beds and ceramics, both ornamental and utilitarian.'

The house was never comfortable or warm – for a long time there was no piped hot water or electricity and it was certainly never smart or glossy – but it was a wonderful playground with an atmosphere typical of the freewheeling 1920s. It was also a jumble of styles: Omega screens and ceramics, reflecting avant-garde French taste, were placed next to Chinese textiles and Persian tiles; drawings by Delacroix were hung next to those by Vanessa Bell's young children, and extreme examples of Victoriana were presented as amusing bad taste.

Popular motifs changed throughout the decade. Figures of dancers and swimmers gave way in the 1920s to nudes, vases of flowers, fruit, musical instruments, swags, medallions and ornaments. Duncan Grant's mythical figures were inspired by the Italian and Greek paganism of E. M. Forster. The popular motifs of the 1930s and 1940s were always more abstract: commas appeared in dark grey on a pale grey background, decorated with white flowers, while black walls were scattered with strong grey geometrics.

Furniture consisted of a mixture of old pieces picked up in local antique shops, and more contemporary items from London designers and the Omega workshops. Everything was painted, not just doors and walls, but baths, radiators, screens and lamps, even the wings of the chickens kept in the yard. Stools were enlivened with needlework seats, mirror frames with embroidery, and tables with tiled tops. Chairs were often cane-backed and painted red in imitation of lacquer; others were covered in needlepoint. Dressing tables were painted or inlaid with marquetry. Pottery was produced by Vanessa and her son Quentin in rose and green, yellow and purple and turquoise, black and red with a light lustre finish.

Yet out of all this diversity came a remarkable and invigorating unity, difficult to explain and impossible to copy. The dining room is painted in a dramatic silvery black, dominated by a large and prettily painted table surrounded by Omega chairs; the sitting room, however, is stencilled and painted in a soft and luminous grey. Also on the ground floor is Vanessa Bell's bedroom, opening on to the garden and bizarrely furnished with a painted bath.

Upstairs, the library is the most striking room. The walls are painted in black and Indian red; the door panels are decorated with two figures bearing baskets, while above and below the window are a dog and a cockerel, both painted by Duncan Grant. The bedrooms all have a distinct individuality and are full of engaging oddities, from a piece of stained glass set into a door to a headboard painted in the form of

Morpheus, God of Sleep, and arresting colour schemes such as yellow ochre and lemon.

Charleston is more than a charming eccentricity; it is unique. Vanessa Bell and Duncan Grant had the courage and the vision to make their own design decisions and to execute them without reference to any received canons of good taste or rule books. Embracing elements from the most disparate sources, Charleston represents all the eclecticism and refreshing liberality of this period of interior design.

Period Decoration Today

A heightened awareness of style in everyday surroundings has brought with it an increased sensitivity to the styles of different eras. While Laura Ashley is known the world over for country cottons and sprig designs, there is another side to their talents – the creation of styles of the past. Many room sets have been designed as exact and specific historic recreations. The results, in living terms, are not as theatrical as might be imagined, more a refreshing change of scene. From the opulent age of the Regency, inspired by George IV's magnificent Royal Pavilion at Brighton, come traditional chinoiserie prints in contemporary colours, while from eighteenth-century India comes a rich interpretation of the paisley pattern. Patterns inspired by the designs of Owen Jones suggest the atmosphere of Victorian times.

At Charleston in Sussex, the home of Vanessa Bell and Duncan Grant for over thirty years, we can see the Bloomsbury style at its most developed. Here everything is treated as a potential vehicle for design, from the chairs and lamps to the tables and pottery. In the sitting room, a trompe l'oeil mural above the fireplace is set against the painted walls, while in the dining room a painted table top plays host to a variety of pieces of pottery designed by Quentin and Vanessa Bell.

Even the exuberance of avant-garde designs of the 1930s has a place within the Laura Ashley collections. In 1986, after a long period of decay and neglect, Charleston farmhouse was opened to the public for the first time. It is not surprising that Laura Ashley should have seen the potential of the colourful designs produced by Vanessa Bell and Duncan Grant. The resulting partnership between Laura Ashley and Charleston was an imaginative one. Seven facsimile fabrics were reproduced for the restored rooms of the house, using large flat-bed printing equipment to reproduce the large repeat in the original designs, and ensuring that the results had an appropriately faded and used look. As a result of this co-operation, Laura Ashley has been allowed to print adaptations of Bell and Grant designs in their own colourways as part of their Bloomsbury Collection, launched in 1987.

In addition, Vanessa Bell's surviving son Quentin, a distinguished potter, has reinterpreted four Charleston designs in the form of a fruit bowl and plate, a lamp-base and a vase, to be produced at the Fulham Pottery by a team of young potters trained by Quentin Bell himself. It is through such projects that tradition is perpetuated, and 'period style' remains a living part of interior decoration.

PERIOD STYLE
Laura Ashley

A glimpse of the elegance of travel in Victorian times with the flavour of the Orient Express. The burgundy and dark green wallpaper, derived from Owen Jones's pattern book, covers the walls of this railway carriage, co-ordinating perfectly with the striped curtains and piped cushions. Even the hat box is given a period flavour.

The re-creation of period styles, rooms in which the past harmoniously meets the present, is another facet of Laura Ashley style. The interiors of the past have become a Pandora's box of inspirational ideas that can enrich and transform the most modern surroundings. Laura Ashley have designed room sets exactly according to historic periods, re-creating colour schemes, fabrics, wallpapers and furnishings in a rich evocation of a bygone era. The results, in living terms, are not as strangely theatrical as might be imagined, more a refreshing change of scene. Alternatively, the atmosphere of the past can be merely suggested, the elegance of the Regency perhaps.

Colours instantly capture the flavour of the time – rich greens and deep reds recall the eighteenth century while fruit pastels evoke the thirties. Prints re-create the effect of traditional damask, watered silks or hand-embroidered needlework. Furnishings from decorative screens to studio pottery can evoke a vanished lifestyle down to the smallest detail.

Period re-creations will appeal to all those who secretly long for the faded richness of the Georgian period, the tasteful stripes of the Regency, the deep-buttoned comfort of Victorian England or the vivacious Bloomsbury of the thirties □

The great pleasure of re-creating period styles lies in educating the eye in the colours and decorative schemes of the past, in hunting for references and inspiration in prints, paintings and contemporary books, and in collecting the antique details which complete the effect. Most Laura Ashley designs are inspired by or taken from period originals, from Georgian designs to those of Charleston in the 1930s. This reconstruction of a Victorian railway carriage shows what can be achieved with the appropriate key elements of wallpaper, curtains and tablecloth.

Spitalfields remains one of the most unspoilt Georgian areas of London today, its narrow streets of houses built by Huguenot silk weavers forced by religious persecution to flee France at the end of the seventeenth century.

The houses are built to a basic plan with a big room in front and a smaller one, like this sitting room, at the back, characterized by a corner fireplace. Delft tiles were a popular feature of fireplaces of the period. Each tile showed an incident from a well-known tale with the idea of prompting story-telling as the family gathered round the fire in the evening. Although only cheap pine panelling was affordable, this was painted a warm russet brown and grained to look like oak, an effect which has been copied here. Floorboards were painted too, as were the planks of the ceiling, which were also often left unplastered as a cheap alternative.

It is against this background that the decorative elements of the room have been carefully assembled. Fabric was the first consideration. A Venetian-inspired cloth was used throughout; its rich damask effect of gold on a subtle tone of green is reminiscent of the exquisite silks the Huguenots themselves wove in the attics of these houses. The pale sheen of the green brings light into the room and the gold plays up the rich patina of the panelling and the luxury of a litter of antique cushions. The chandelier is Georgian, but other elements, though old, are eclectic and comfortable: a daybed with fat bolsters, a Queen Anne wing chair, and a gateleg table with a creamy lace shawl for a tablecloth. An Aubusson rug on the floor adds its beautifully faded colours to the evocative look of the room. A simple fall of muslin is all that is needed to shade the sun. At night, the shutters are drawn and the occupants are completely enclosed in russet panelling.

This lively dining room is the perfect example of how a painting can be used as direct inspiration in re-creating a period room. The painting is of the Ruspoli family taking breakfast in their Italian *palazzo* in 1807.

The first aspect to consider is the colour scheme: the rich moss green, crimson and navy of the Ruspoli room are modified to fir green and terracotta, while the navy in the carpet is replaced by a ground of sand, though its terracotta figuring and broad, ornate border are similar to the original. For the wallpaper, the serpentine form of an exuberant design inspired by an eighteenth-century print echoes the feathery plumes of the paper in the painting.

Marbling like that used in the Palazzo Ruspoli is enjoying a current vogue and you can employ professionals, attempt it yourself or use a *faux* marble paper. This marbled dado incorporates the Vitruvian scroll motif and the gilded moulding of the original, while an amusing painted mural is a faithful trompe l'oeil imitation of the blue and gold panel above the fireplace.

The period chairs are upholstered in broad, vivid stripes of fir green and terracotta, wide stripes being a typical pattern on dining-chair upholstery at this date. The table is draped in an antique white damask cloth complemented by napkins, place mats and cosies in a fine floral print; silver egg cups are a nice reminder of the Ruspolis' more princely breakfast.

A screen has been introduced, its pointed Gothic outline adding an eclectic note, but its striped fabric covering integrates it with the overall scheme. It provides a decorative disguise for the breakfast dishes that have not yet been cleared away.

This delightful room takes its cue from the print rooms that were the vogue at the end of the eighteenth century, when gentlemen of means would return from their Grand Tour of Italy laden with cultural souvenirs, among them the equivalent of today's picture postcards – prints. The purpose of the tour being classical education, these were generally engravings after ancient or Renaissance works of art. Ladies in particular took to papering the walls of small sitting rooms and dressing rooms with a profusion of such prints, framed and decorated with printed swags and bows, almost always against a pale yellow or pink background. Mrs Philip Lybbe Powys, in her diary of 1771, remarks on a room at Fawley Court that was lined with 'the most beautiful pink India paper, adorned with very good prints'.

Wallpaper rendered to look like silk, to match the upholstery and curtain fabrics, was just coming into fashion at this time, often used with borders – a combination that was to last well into the nineteenth century. Here, moiré wallpaper is used with an architectural acanthus border, itself of print-like appearance, at cornice, dado and skirting level. The moiré is picked up in the unusual pelmet design, edged in aquamarine braid, taken from Sheraton's pelmet designs for the Chinese Drawing Room at the Brighton Pavilion. The curtains below are in watercolour-stripes of white, apricot and aquamarine.

The fine lines of the furniture, the prettiness of the rose trellis rug and the suggestion of music, all serve to make this a refined and elegant room.

A light, airy, eighteenth-century elegance pervades this English breakfast room with its sense of relaxed informality. Traditionally, the breakfast room is not only a place in which to eat, but an informal sitting room in which members of the family can gather at any time of day in comfortable surroundings. To create such an atmosphere demands a form of decoration far less ornate than that of a more conventional dining room. Here, such an effect has been achieved using an attractive large floral print in pinks, greens, smoky blues and browns, whose origins lie in English country house fabrics of the 1820s. Graceful, full-length curtains frame the breakfast area, taking up this master print in which cushions and chairs are also covered, edged and piped with a rose-coloured border. A delicate complementary design of stylized pink tulips on a stippled ground of cool mint green is used for the window seat banquettes and blinds.

Light floods the large bay windows, and with the pale tones of the woodwork, carries the green of the surrounding countryside into the room to give the feeling of a fresh spring morning.

All the romantic associations of the Regency era are encapsulated in Robert Smirke's watercolour of Madame Recamier's bedchamber. The fringed bedhangings of white Indian muslin, embroidered with gold stars, are suspended by a gilded coronet, fringed to match the drapery, while the walls are swathed in violet silk, topped by a silk pelmet.

Such a luxurious retreat can be re-created anywhere. The use of such a simple hanging in voile, cotton or chintz can completely transform the most ordinary of bedrooms, immediately making them appear softer and more inviting. This farmhouse bedroom now exudes all the romance of the Regency era without having lost any of its rural charm. A simple paper border in a mid-nineteenth-century print of floral bouquets was used with a co-ordinating wallpaper print of cherry flowers with light green leaves on a white ground. The bed is hung with a voluminous drape of white voile suspended from a simply constructed corona, lending it all the appearance of a romantic, early nineteenth-century day bed.

Even the bedroom of a château, with its classical proportions and fine panelling, can benefit from the decorative style of the Regency. Pale green moiré wallpaper is complemented by the delicate mouldings on door and panelling, also picked out in the same pale shade of green. The polished mahogany bed dates from this period, its fitted bolster and cover relieved by an elegant burgundy and green border. The fall of muslin that graces the bed is held back with brass rosettes, and the window drapery carries through this same theme, diffusing the soft afternoon light.

Contemporary books are just as useful as pictures in revealing the design ideas of a period. J. C. Loudon's *Encyclopedia of Cottage, Farm and Villa Architecture* of 1833 suggests that a Victorian hall should be 'gloomy' to act as a foil to the rooms leading off it. Consequently, a dark but rich colour scheme of burgundy, navy and sand was chosen, with a distinctive wallpaper and an egg and dart border based on a design by Owen Jones. A few items of furniture suffice: a looking-glass to give a sense of space, two shell-backed chairs and a little table on which, at one time, a silver salver would have received visitors' calling cards.

The hall opens onto the drawing room where two of its colours, crimson and sand, are the basis for a sumptuous decorative scheme. The geometric wallpaper, also inspired by an Owen Jones design, echoes the paper in the hall. The carpet, crimson on a fawn ground, is copied from a popular type of early nineteenth-century chenille rug, while skirting boards are grained in imitation of mahogany.

The deep-buttoned sofa and armchairs are upholstered in a rich and beautiful crimson sateen (the typical Victorian drawing room fabric) and the curtains are in the same fabric, as recommended by Loudon.

In a period interior, the appropriate decorative objects are essential in creating an authentic atmosphere. Period pieces like the early Argand oil lamp with its Wedgwood drum, a coal 'receiver', a tapestry bell-pull to hang at one side of the fireplace, and a lacquered firescreen all help to complete the final picture. Even the flowers have been arranged in the bunch-like Victorian manner as opposed to the more triangular bouquets of today. Knowing *how* to arrange the room is just as important as knowing what to put in it.

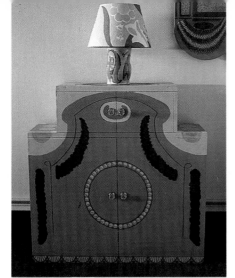

The unmistakeable blithe spirit of Bloomsbury prevades this room – a re-creation of the Music Room designed by artists Vanessa Bell and Duncan Grant, and exhibited at the Lefevre Gallery in London in 1932.

Everything is decorated in a very freely-expressed, painterly style – fabrics, mirrors, ceramics and furniture. On the walls hang a pair of flower paintings in which the frames are a continuation of the picture; cut in loops to emphasize the drapery, the frames are inset with quirky little mirrors at the top. A cupboard is painted with architectural features and various off-the-cuff motifs. Above the fireplace hangs a gloriously eccentric mirror, again with mirrors set into its frame and painted with spontaneous strokes of colour.

Bloomsbury style stands for joyful, undiluted decoration – the handmade, homemade and the individual. The border design used for the pelmet, and also for the banquette and chairs, is just such a piece of irreverence, gaily combined with a design of fruit and leaves on curtains and upholstery in colours of grey, cowslip, apricot and black. The stylized rug is a scaled-down version of an original design by Vanessa Bell, while the fruit bowl and plate were designed specially for Laura Ashley by Quentin Bell, son of Vanessa and a potter in the same unfettered tradition.

This small sitting room in West London, with its supremely relaxed atmosphere, takes its inspiration from Charleston, a farmhouse in the rolling Sussex countryside that was home to the talented circle of artists that called themselves the Bloomsbury Group. During the 1920s and '30s, the entire house was treated as one great canvas, tirelessly embellished by its owners with paint, stencils and glaze. A childlike appreciation of surfaces 'dressed up' showed itself in a carefree form of decoration, informal yet full of the creative enjoyment of colour and shape.

The whimsical spirit of Charleston is re-created here with a wave-patterned wallpaper, designed by Vanessa Bell, that brings a warmth to the room with its soft straw-coloured tones. The pelmet fabric, framing the expansive window that leads onto the balcony beyond, has all the confident rhythmic flair of naive Bloomsbury designs, and is amusingly repeated as a skirt for the window seat and as matching tie-backs for the curtains. Simple terracotta pots are filled with a splash of red and pink geraniums. The armchair and sofa wear their covers lightly, contributing to the comfortable ease of the room – a fitting reminder of the charmingly animated, gaily coloured and perpetually youthful style from which it derives.

The nursery is the ideal room for a thirties look: bright and cheerful with plain and practical furniture that can stand up to any amount of wear and tear. It was a pragmatic decade, and for most people economy was the watchword of the day, reflected in simple, stylized motifs and a functional but cosy sense of style.

Several features instantly determine the room's period feel. First, the colour combination of pastel yellow walls with a vibrant contrast of smoke-blue on picture rail, wooden pelmet and fireplace. These light, bright colours give the room an upbeat, jazzy feel.

Cartoon characters were just becoming fashionable in the thirties. Here, on a fitted carpet of the same smoke blue tone as the woodwork, a pink rug sports these motifs, also seen on the child's gramaphone and simply-framed pictures. Sofa and armchair are in classic, soft and rounded twentieth-century shapes, completely covered with fabric. Freehand stripes in pretty pastel colours give them a casual feel (the sofa is charmingly reduced to child-size proportions). The curtains are in a similar, but finer, pastel stripe, whereas cushions and a doll's tea-table cloth are in a splashy pattern of softly- coloured, stylized flowers.

Basketwork furniture was popular in the thirties, especially Lloyd loom chairs, often painted white but straw-coloured here, and given a comfortable look with channel-quilted liners that match the sofa stripes. Essential nostalgia is provided by the overmantel mirror, and the stylized wireless.

MODERN

STYLE

MODERN STYLE
Past Traditions

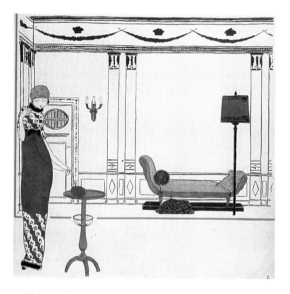

Although it dates from a few years before, this fashionable interior of a Paris apartment has many of the features which became popular during the 1920s. The walls are plain but for simple, painted Neo-classical columns and a dado. The chaise longue is redolent of the Regency and Empire revivals, and the influence of the Ballets Russes, which was soon to sweep the world of interior decoration.

The very words 'modern style' conjure up images of austere, clean lines, neutral colour schemes of white and black or vibrant primary colours, minimal decoration and the sleek new materials of the twentieth century – chrome, glass and steel. Modernism took the radical step of challenging the existing order; in turn, it prompted a great diversity of reactionary styles which have made positive design statements of their own. Today, modern technology and materials allow even greater freedom of expression within interior decoration.

Where do the sources of the twentieth-century interior lie? The early decades saw an extraordinary flowering of invention in interior design that was international in its scope. Design took precedence over decoration, function gained the upper hand over ornament, the city became the focus of attention rather than the countryside, and new materials and techniques surpassed the old.

The legacy of modern design is the soothing calm of uncluttered space, an emphasis on classic line and shape, the reduction to essentials. But a room can be much more than 'a machine for living in', especially when the best of modern design is combined with the pleasures of decoration and an ageless air of ease and comfort □

The first major turning point in twentieth-century culture was 1918, the year in which the First World War ended. A decimated Europe fell back exhausted from four years of unprecedented horror. Those who had survived wanted complete and radical change, an abrupt end to an old order and an immediate start to the new. There existed a belief in the divine power of machinery and technology and its ability to work a new set of miracles, transforming the conditions of life.

The Bauhaus Look

But nothing in history works so neatly or absolutely, and many of the fresh artistic initiatives of the early 1920s in fact had their roots in the pre-war era. In domestic architecture, for instance, the houses built by Frank Lloyd Wright (1869–1959) in America as early as the 1890s, look far ahead of their time in their breaking-down of divisions between exterior and interior, and in their low spreading open-plan rooms, picture windows and ceiling-high brick fireplaces. Wright's ideas had a great effect in Europe, particularly his insistence that 'it is quite impossible to consider the buildings as one thing, its furnishings another'. In Vienna Josef Hoffmann and Adolf Loos continued his spirit of stark simplicity and unity in architecture, while in Germany the young Walter Gropius produced a programme for the mass production of small houses using standardized parts. The machine-made and the minimal dominated the thinking of the avant-garde: 'one thing instead of many things,' as Frank Lloyd Wright put it, 'a great thing instead of a collection of small ones'.

From these seeds grew the first great post-war design movement, that of the Bauhaus, an art school founded by Gropius in 1919. All the decorative arts such as furniture, pottery, metal work and graphics, as well as fashion, were taught by the leading figures in these fields, all dedicated to Gropius's 'desire for a universal style of design stemming from and expressive of an integral society and culture.' The marriage of aesthetics and geometry in the concept of 'function' defined the Bauhaus look, and it has been a dominating trend in interior design ever since. Bauhaus products like the tubular steel chair designed by Marcel Breuer in 1925, influenced by a method of curving metals used in aircraft construction, are still in use today. This was followed in 1926 by a cantilevered chair in tubular steel and leather. The interiors of the Bauhaus itself were exemplary. The Director's Room, for instance, showed unrelieved wall surfaces, tubular aluminium light fittings, and wall hangings woven out of a mixture of natural and synthetic fibres. Fitted furniture was another innovation. Militantly set against decoration and excess, the Bauhaus represented the most coherent attempt to forge a creative future for design in the machine age.

At the same time as the Bauhaus was pushing forward frontiers in Germany, similar developments were being pursued elsewhere in Europe. Russia, in the wake of the Revolution of 1917, saw the emergence of movements like Constructivism and Suprematism, which proclaimed the art of the machine as a political statement. They expressed themselves primarily through architecture and industrial design, employing the new materials of steel, plastic and concrete. In Holland, the interiors and furniture designed by Gerrit Rietveld translated the uncompromisingly abstract paintings of Piet Mondrian into the Schroder House, built in Utrecht in 1925, and the famous 'red-blue' armchair, with its severe slab-like seat. In Italy, the Fascist regime associated itself with a design style that approached modern neo-classicism – bold and impressive, with marble, glass and lavish veneers.

Léon Bakst was the doyen of stage set and costume designers in the Paris of the 1920s. He worked extensively for Diaghilev, helping to create the tremendously influential style known as 'Ballets Russes'. This watercolour by Bakst, his design for a eunuch's costume for the ballet Scheherezade, *shows the abandoned line and sense of colour which soon began to have an effect on the fashionable interiors of London, Paris, New York and Berlin.*

The Influence of Art Deco

Such modernism did not appeal to the same extent in France. The Paris of Picasso, Braque, Léger, Gertrude Stein and Scott Fitzgerald was a brighter, warmer and more eclectic place. The design impact of Diaghilev's Ballets Russes – exotic and extravagant, coloured in rich

Classic styles of design have the ability to stand the test of time. This contemporary apartment, once the home of that connoisseur of the twenties Martin Battersby, exudes a feeling for that period. The wall covering is a grid of silver and gold, suggestive of the Viennese artists of the day. On the wall hangs a picture by Léon Bakst, and before it stands a vase by Neilz, flanked in the window recesses by a pair of vases designed by Dunand. All these designers played an influential part in shaping the interior of the 1920s.

greens and scarlets, purples and oranges – was immense, overpowering the mannered swirling lines of Art Nouveau designs of the 1890s with its bold primitivism and uninhibited energy. Cubism and Dada were major new forces in painting, vogues for primitive carving and the friezes of Ancient Egypt emerged, and in music jazz was all the rage. These elements together formed the style known as Art Deco.

Art Deco's high point came with the 1925 Paris Exhibition of Decorative and Industrial Arts, where the pavilion of furniture designer Jacques-Emile Ruhlmann was one of the most magnificent: in a circular salon with a huge crystal chandelier, walls were covered with a silken pattern of flowers, vases and birds. Elsewhere wrought-iron work, mural panels and lacquer were in evidence. Sophistication and luxury was the tone. The famous glass-maker René Lalique created a stunning dining room with beige and grey marbled walls inlaid with silver and white, and a ceiling in which the lighting was concealed behind glass beams and coffers. Art Deco also favoured new and recherché materials such as ambyona, olive and ebony woods; sharkskin and parchment panels; aluminium and bakelite plastic. Surviving interiors embodying this trend outside France include the Strand Palace Hotel and Savoy Theatre in London, and the Radio City

On a table designed by Ruhlmann lie an assortment of decorative objects, stamped with '20s style: cigarette cases, an ashtray and a delightfully kitsch lamp by Roland in the form of a dancer.

Music Hall in New York. Brought into the home, it spelt colour, with much streamlining, and geometrical patterns of zigzags and circles. But it was a fashionable style that was soon to be dismissed for its cheap, 'of the moment' image. Art Deco was satirized by Osbert Lancaster as consisting of 'a couple of handmade earthenware pots of inconvenient shape and offensive green glaze, filled perhaps with a spray of Cape gooseberries . . . round the top of the wall a frieze of painted water-lilies in a complicated and sinuous pattern that was repeated as likely as not in tiles or beaten copper over the fireplace.'

The Beauty of the Machine

In architecture, the most significant name of the period was that of Le Corbusier, pseudonym of Charles Jeanneret (1887–1965). His studies had taken place mostly in Germany and Austria where he was influenced by nascent modernist ideas. Out of his early enthusiasm for the motor car and aeroplane was born his understanding of the beauty of the machine, which he believed could be adapted to provide a model for a perfect living environment. His notorious description of a house as 'a machine for living in' sums up his architectural philosophy. In his *Manual of the Dwelling*, published in 1923, he noted his requirements for such a house:

> . . . a bathroom looking south, one of the largest rooms in the house or flat . . . One wall to be entirely glazed . . . demand bare walls in your bedroom, your living room and your dining room. Built-in fittings to take the place of furniture which is expensive to buy, takes up too much room, and needs looking after . . . If you can, put the kitchen at the top of the house to avoid unpleasant smells . . . Teach your children that a house is only habitable when it is full of light and air, when the floors and walls are clear. To keep your floors in order eliminate heavy furniture and thick carpets.

Most of the twenty-six buildings he constructed during the 1920s were domestic houses and all contain his trademarks: large horizontal windows to catch the natural sunlight; an open-plan interior with movable partitions separating living and dining spaces; and the lack of any attempt to mask major structural features. In later years Le Corbusier concentrated on apartment blocks, of which post-war 'high-rise' flats are a debased descendant.

Following the Stock Market crash of 1929 and the subsequent economic depression, the mood of the 1930s was less hopeful and enthusiastic than that of the frenetic 1920s, with its gramophones, cocktails, cabarets, and risqué dances such as the Charleston and Black Bottom. As the *Decorative Year Book* of 1932 put it:

The 'jazz' period may be said to be over. Extravagance and grotesquerie were the spicing and seasoning demanded during the hectic phase of 'post-war', which was filled with the feverishness of the war itself, and the high spirits produced by its termination. All this is on the wane.

In the 1930s, the emphasis in interior design was laid on the 'streamlined', a catchword which first took hold in 1932 when Norman Bel Geddes published his book of industrial design philosophy, *Horizons*. From vacuum cleaners to pencil sharpeners, razors to toothpaste tubes, cigarette packets to refrigerators, everything in this American variant of modernism ministered to the convenience of the consumer and encouraged a materialism unparalleled since the mid-Victorian era.

The Age of Utility

In 1939 the world once again trudged to war and any aesthetic concerns with the decorative aspects of interior furnishing were entirely subordinated to a basic wartime functionalism. Furniture and fabrics were strictly rationed, and production was channelled into the war effort, weapons, uniforms, and military equipment all reflecting 'machine modernism'.

From 1943, under the close supervision of Gordon Russell, the British Board of Trade began to manufacture 'utility' furniture. The origins of this style lie with Russell's own experiments in the 1930s, in which he

ABOVE *This interior, designed by Frank Gutmann in 1930, provides a good example of the sort of colour scheme which would have been popular during the 1930s. The deliberately long, low shape of the room is coloured in a symphony of pale blue, cream and apricot; quiet, Mediterranean colours that reflect the geographical origins of Le Corbusier's machine à habiter.*

LEFT AND ABOVE RIGHT *Design in the 1930s was characterized by a preoccupation with light, and the elimination of unnecessary detail. However, there was no corresponding lack of fine materials and solid building methods. Here in this streamlined living room, designed in 1937, only the very best was used: English maple, rosewood veneer, the finest white leather and elegantly sculpted aluminium.*

had attempted to reconcile a William Morris-inspired desire for good craftsmanship with the obvious advantages of efficient, mechanized production. The essence of the operation was the saving of raw materials, without sacrificing the basic tenets of good design. A shortage of wood meant that there was extra reliance on new materials and techniques, such as the moulding of plywood and aluminium. It was a requirement perfectly suited to the spirit of modernism.

In effect, 'utility' served both to encourage British furniture design and to make available to a far wider public than ever before a relatively higher quality of product than that to which they had been accustomed. In this respect Russell might be said to have realized a part of Morris's Arts and Crafts ideal: however, the actual designs dated badly, and were drab rather than classic in style. The post-war years were bleak, and utility furniture was followed by prefabricated housing, which had been pioneered by Gropius forty years earlier. Decoration was dominated by escapist motifs of fairgrounds and circuses, and wallpaper was revived as a cheap way of livening up interiors. The glitter of America, from the chrome-plated sports car to the wonder of nylon stockings, seemed much more attractive.

The Fifties Interior

The era of frugality ended in 1951, and the assertion of a new brightness and efficiency spread through the many exhibitions and competitions associated with the Festival of Britain. The style was often described as 'contemporary' and can be seen as a simplification and popularization of the inter-war modernist school. The fabric designs of Lucienne Day and the furniture of Ernest Race are typical of the period. So, too, was the emphasis on the manageable domestic interior in which you could 'do-it-yourself'. Attention was focused on kitchen furniture and planning, facilitated by the advent of practical plastic surfaces.

Throughout the Western world homes were getting smaller, and the semi-detached or terraced house was being left behind in favour of the tower blocks of post-war reconstruction policies. In decoration, ordinary homes moved further towards the urban and masculine, the stark and straightforward. The most important manifestation of this was the spread of open-plan design: in 1950 the design commentator George Nelson noted in his influential book *Tomorrow's House* the demise of 'the little partitioned cubicles called rooms.' The open-plan principle gave the smaller house or converted flat a sense of increased space and suited the new informality that was growing in family life. Built-in furniture systems were now prevalent and the concept of the kitchen-diner came into fashion. Another feature of the time was the picture window, and central heating finally replaced the open fire.

The Festival of Britain, the symbol of which is shown here, gave many young designers the chance to show off their ideas. For many it represented the start of a new era of post-war positivism and led the way towards the freer experimentation of the 1960s.

Elements of the decorative style of the 1950s can be seen in this London drawing room, incorporated into an eclectic scheme that is both personal and sophisticated. The pale colours of the walls and matching bookcase, the cream rug and above all the cloud-shaped table hint subtly at the clean, uncluttered lines of 1950s design that originated in Scandinavia and became popular after the Festival of Britain.

In response to the general reduction of scale in living conditions, furniture decreased in size, and the advice of Le Corbusier to abandon heavy wooden furniture for small lighter items, framed in the new alloys, was followed. As early as 1939 Hans Coray had designed stacking chairs in tubular steel, a design still in production in the 1980s. However, it was a predominant American furniture designer, Charles Eames, who pioneered the American-style stacking chair moulded in plastic, as well as a contemporary version of the traditional club chair. The *Daily Mail Ideal Home Book* for 1951–2 described the general look as having 'an air of simpleness, almost rusticity, which is deceptive in such graceful and sophisticated stuff. The chairs and tables all stand on outspread tapered legs like a ballet dancer on her points ... The idea is to give a feeling of wider floor space in small rooms – floating, the designers call it.'

Another very popular range of 1950s contemporary furniture was 'G-plan', launched as a reinterpretation of Russell's utility style and incorporating such features as shelf systems and room dividers: 'make your own design choices and assemble your furniture from kits' was the message in the high street store.

To most people in Britain, this contemporary style, with all its breezy and cheery brightness, represented the ultimate in modern living, and even the craze for do-it-yourself encapsulated the positive, energetic, unstuffy spirit which was thought to characterize the 1950s. It cut across all levels of society. Plants, small pictures and contemporary ornaments filled every house, with emphasis on the crisp and sharply angled. Lighting became openly and obviously directional; bright primary colours contrasted with more muted tones. Simple geometric shapes like stars, circles and hexagons, all of which could be easily cut on a jig, were prominent. Wallpaper became more sophisticated, not only at the upper end of the market, where hessian weaves and silk linings were popular, but for the ordinary kitchen and bathroom, where washable and steam-resistant vinyl papers proved eminently practical. The bathroom, in particular, came into its own as, in design journalist John Prizeman's words, 'a space in which to relax, think, listen to music, look at pictures, read, dream, drink, eat grapes, exercise and sing'!

The other dominant influence in the 1950s continued to be that of America, and the values and artefacts of American mass culture from Hollywood dreams to motorbikes and transistor radios. The greatest social change was wrought by the advent of television (often framed in a veneered cabinet) which caused people to spend more time at home and re-focused the furnishings of every living room.

Some of the best designs of the era undoubtedly emanated from Scandinavia, a part of Europe which had quietly kept true to its folk traditions of clean lines, simple wooden interiors and sterling crafts-manship. It was Sweden that led the way; later in the decade it was Denmark's turn, as manifested in such timeless pieces as Arne Jacobsen's 'Ant' chair, which transformed austere functionalism into genuine elegance. The Finnish approach was altogether bolder, and notable for its brightly-coloured textiles. Against the disposability of so much Anglo-American design – 'high-tech', but low in finish and durability – the Scandinavian influence was a return to reason.

Italian Design

It was clear, however, by the end of the 1950s, that something had to replace the flimsiness of contemporary style, and that Modernism would have to become more dynamic if its impetus was to continue. The answer came neither from confident Britain, nor from that trend-setter of the past, France; nor did it originate in Germany, the cradle of modernism, or even streamlined America. The answer lay in Italy, birthplace of the Renaissance.

After the Second World War, Italy underwent a violent backlash against the 1930s styles associated with Mussolini and his fascist policies. Italian design in the 1950s had a compensating soft and rounded quality, best summed up in the term 'organic'. It is seen everywhere, from the Olivetti typewriter to Gio Ponti's coffee machines and to the sleek wasp-like line of that archetypal symbol of late 1950s teenage affluence, the Vespa scooter. Cassina, the furniture company, was responsible for producing a number of important new ideas including Ponti's '*superleggera*' chair of 1957. Given the wealth of talent and energy in the field, it is not surprising that by the beginning of the 1960s, Italy had become the world's leading furniture exporter.

The Italian design revolution heralded the exploitation of a wide variety of new materials – bent and moulded plywood, sheet metals, rods, glass, foam rubber and plastic laminates. The potential of the latter was notably exploited by Gino Colombini who, between 1955 and 1960 in his work for the Kartell company, gave real aesthetic weight to such everyday household objects as wall brackets, vegetable baskets and colanders.

Gradually the new Italian elegance spread across Europe: as the Florentine designer Andrea Brazi observed, 'even the smallest joiner's shop soon learnt how to work bar counters that looked like Gio Ponti's own designs.'

The Sixties

Italy set the pace for the 1960s, but the changes in that decade were generated not so much by deliberate theorizing as by a social phenomenon: the rise of youth, youth-spending and youth-style. Colin Macinnes's novel *Absolute Beginners*, published in 1959, heralds the birth of a new teenage 'bohemian' style, casual yet discriminating. 'I've

The 1960s and '70s saw a greater social freedom than had ever been known before, which was manifested in all things including interior design. This painting by David Hockney of the designer Ossie Clark and his wife includes a number of early '70s decorating motifs: the plain white plastic coffee table, the French louvred shutters, the heavy shag rug on the floor and Mr Clark's tubular chair.
At the same time, Laura Ashley was beginning to make an impact on the interior decorating market with her soon-to-be famous combination of country style furnishings – simple ceramic lamps, and of course wallpapers in one-colour designs with a distinctly rural flavour.

decorated it all in what I call anti-contemptuous style, i.e. ancient Aunt Fanny wallpapers I got from some leftovers in a paint shop in the Portobello Road,' announces the central character. 'I've got a bed too, a triple one, and the usual chair and table; but no other chairs and instead a lot of cushions spread out on the floor and on top of what is my only luxury, a fitted carpet . . . The only other objects are my record-player, my pocket transistor radio, and stacks of discs and books that I've collected.'

As sales of scooters, motorbikes and radios rocketed, furnishings were quick to follow. But they were not bought in the traditional units of three-piece suites and double-thickness curtains. To the youth generation of the sixties it was clear that surroundings, like clothes and possessions, reflected not only moral character but social status. Style mattered; the message of Pop culture was one of freedom and experimentation, with less value placed on the material. Its influence could be seen strongly in interior furnishings – nothing solemn, nothing permanent.

Capitalizing on this thinking, Terence Conran opened his first shop in the Fulham Road, London, and overnight became the leading exponent of the philosophy of 'packaged good taste'. *The Sunday Times* observed of its opening: 'there is a growing feeling, particularly amongst young shoppers, that they want to make shopping for the home an impulsive, gay affair.'

London was the hub of the 'swinging sixties', frenetic but fun. Fashions changed constantly: mini skirts became maxi length; colours changed from purple to turquoise. In interiors, crazes came and went at a similarly furious pace; one famous overnight sensation was Peter Murdoch's spotted paper chair of 1965. Certain themes and trends lasted longer than others: 'futuristic' silver was one, with its chrome silver spotlights, polished steel furniture and even silvery pillow covers; white wood furniture, although difficult to keep clean, was a hallmark of the sixties that is still popular today. The Italian Joe Colombo had considerable success with his strong but eccentric designs for a fold-away bed, a spider lamp, 'Elda' chair and perspex desk lights. Quasar Khan created inflatable chairs in transparent plastic; Zanuso designed radical new seating concepts such as the inflatable 'blow chair' and the soft 'Sacco' chair, filled with balls of polystyrene.

Outside the Pop culture, there was a campaign among the more expensive and exclusive interior decorators to raise standards and to stop cutting corners for the sake of effect. John Fowler made careful studies of 'correct' period fabrics and colour schemes in his superb and pioneering work on the restoration of country house interiors; David Hicks's reputation was for bold mixtures of the old and new, set in rooms which startlingly juxtaposed colours and textures. The art of interior decoration, he claimed, was 'the art of achieving the maximum with the minimum'. In lesser hands, it looked mannered and cold, and through the medium of glossy magazines it was debased into a standard chic style of which Quentin Crisp drily observed: 'the higher the income bracket, the lower the furniture.' Conran's chain of stores has continued to lead the market in bright, glossy and convenient interior design.

From the mid 1960s, there was some relief from the unremitting noise, colour and energy of Pop culture in the shape of a series of period revivals. For the young, it was a taste for Victoriana which coincided with the cluttered visual look associated with the hippy 'flower power' movement; for the middle classes, it was Regency striped wallpaper and reproduction Georgian elegance; and for the intellectually enlightened, a light-hearted obsession with kitsch.

Modernism Today

Modernism has lived on, not only in the 'high tech' style identified with New York loft living, which makes use of scaffolding, factory lights, car seats, metal storage racks and rubber floors, but in the broader international movement, known as 'post-modernism'. Initially an architectural style realized by American architects such as Michael Graves and Charles Jencks, it has resurrected a role in design for pattern, detail and decoration, while making full use of new building and manufacturing techniques. Among interior designers who had adapted its implications to furnishings, the Italian Ettore Sottsass is outstanding. Admitting influences from sources as disparate as early American Pop culture and ancient mystical religions, Sottsass's designs, such as the 'Tahiti' table lamp of 1981, are colourful, intriguing and witty, emphasizing sculptural qualities and the inter-relationship of adjoining planes.

New Directions

Cool elegance, the clean, uncluttered lines of modern design, the smooth materials of modern technology were not everyone's ideal in interior decoration; nor was this an appropriate style for all living environments. It was this realization that provided the key to Laura Ashley's early success. Prettiness, fun, nostalgia and comfort were ushered back into the design and decoration fold. Yet in their use of bold colours, abstract patterns and clean, elegant lines they have taken up the best of modernist principles, and given them a broader appeal, proving that modernism can be stylishly integrated into the family home.

LEFT *The eclecticism of interior decoration during the 'swinging sixties' is apparent in David Hicks's famous tablescapes. Here he blends the traditional motifs of obelisks and urns, which became his trademark, with an avant-garde painting and a chair upholstered in a striking black and white 'op art' design.*

ABOVE *More mainstream than the work of David Hicks was that of John Fowler, who decorated interiors such as the living room of Nancy Lancaster in a calm and slightly* déshabillé *country house style which was to last through the 1960s to become a predominant style of 1980s decoration.*

MODERN STYLE
Laura Ashley

Laura Ashley have never strived to look 'modern', to create 'modern design'. Instead, their aims have been to create designs for modern *living*. A contemporary interior does not have to be formed from chrome, glass, plastic and tubular steel. For Laura Ashley, modern style is a cool, sophisticated look where decoration is not sacrificed to design but happily co-exists with it. It is a style that is at home anywhere in the world.

Timeless, neutral patterns adapt to modern apartment and traditional house alike. The clean lines of classic stripes, the geometric patterns of a tiled floor, instantly evoke a contemporary atmosphere. Blocks of bright colour are controlled by the coolness of crisp white woodwork, and Roman blinds give windows a smart, neat outline. Loose, painterly floral prints are equally suitable for a modern interior while retaining a certain Englishness that is echoed in print names such as 'Brighton Rock' or 'Cricket Stripe'. Rooms are uncluttered and balanced, yet do not appear austere.

Using the technology of a modern age, Laura Ashley have developed decorative ideas that are entirely appropriate to the relaxed informality of modern life, stylishly integrating the best of twentieth-century design into the family home □

We are a stylish breed, loving style for style's sake and style with a strong sense of history, but we also recognize a specifically modern look, characterized by light-filled rooms with clean lines and a fresh eye on colour. To the arts of other ages we have added the ingenious art of distilling the maximum elegance from an economy of space in rooms which often perform several functions. We rely, as here, on confident, uncluttered effects: a big pot of plain privet, marbled skirting, bold stripes, a delicious sense of colour.

A few simple, stunning effects, often repeated for added emphasis, give this room its modern character. Most important of these is the set of three floor-length windows that dominate one wall and provide an excess of that most desirable modern luxury – light. They are completely surrounded with white-painted woodwork in contrast to the soft apricot walls, which makes them stand out in one block even though the gallery – an eyrie to sleep in – cuts across one window.

The colour scheme is simplified to a play of light grey and white on mellow apricot. Both sofas are covered in an apricot fabric which echoes the walls; both tables are covered in wide-striped grey and white cotton. They provide a simple counterpoint for one another. The print on cushions, sofa stool and festoon blinds, unites all three colours in one design, a blithe print of a huffing and puffing West Wind, seen against freely sketched grey clouds on white. Invested with great freedom of spirit is a second print of apricot flowers on white, scribbled with grey. This covers dining chairs and the slip cover on the larger table. An edging on cushions and cover of ruched grey bias binding is an elegant detail. The cornice is one of the most inspired features of the room. It is picked out in apricot and grey, not only to unify the colour scheme, but to reflect the movement and freshness of the prints in the room below.

A talent for simplicity is the touchstone of a modern lifestyle, perfectly expressed in this contemporary living room at Port Grimaud by the Mediterranean. It is a classless room, neither rich nor poor but unaffected and charming; a case of modern sophistication meeting the earthiness of Provence. It has the emphatic linear forms beloved of today: the low lines of the white coffee table and sofa, the solid steps and the lattice pattern of the window. It also has the whitewashed walls and terracotta tiles of a Provençal farmhouse, a corner cupboard decked with pretty china, and plain kitchen chairs which give it a peasant feel – the clean lines of the modern dovetail neatly into rustic sparseness.

Unadulterated light, the chief decorative feature of many modern houses, pours in through the French windows. Fresh-striped curtains are suspended from a simple white pole on white curtain rings. Apart from white, the transparency of glass and the natural tones of terracotta and wood, there are only two colours in the room: bright mustard and sapphire blue. The sofa, which is simply a stylishly beaded set of storage drawers with sitting space on top, has blue and white striped seat and back cushions with cornflower-sprigged yellow scatter cushions. The yellow and blue are cleverly picked up in the striped paper which lines the corner cupboard. A modern perspective is seen once more in the objects grouped around the staircase – a particularly modern aesthetic.

The drama of this Florida courtyard arises from its vaulted ceiling supported on columns, and the grand entrance stairway that descends into it. Bold, rhetorical devices are needed to play up its sense of theatre, and strong colours and pattern that will not be drowned by its spaciousness. Black, white, grey and crimson are used. In a climate like this, a courtyard is loved for its coolness, which both the ceramic surface and bold pattern of black and white tiles accentuate. Ceiling, walls and staircase are whitewashed and left completely bare. On one side a series of arches leads onto the garden. Grey and white striped curtains can be drawn across the French windows below to subdue the midday sun, leaving elegant Diocletian windows above. Young trees in white tubs add to the sense of shade with their whispering leaves.

The table in the centre of the hall is designed to catch the eye of wandering passersby and make them linger. It is draped with a full-length cloth in a stylized pattern of grey and crimson. The staircase is a well of white against which the richness of crimson window pelmets in the same fretwork design and the delicacy of the wrought-iron balusters stand out. The filigree effect of fine wrought-iron is continued in candlestand, sconces and chandelier. For a suitably grand effect crimson ropes of twisted satin are draped from antique bronze lions heads. A sense of the fun, as well as the richness, to be gained from using antiques in this way gives an informal air to an otherwise imposing room.

Candid, clear colour is the keynote of this tiny, vivacious sitting room in a Brighton seaside hut. A candy striped paper lines the room and sets the tone of fresh prettiness that is picked up in the blue and white striped tablecloths and the pointillist canvas that is the backdrop to the entire scene. The blue, pink, white and straw yellow tones of the room are all mirrored in the picture. These are colours the Impressionists would have loved.

Wickerwork chairs with cushions are immensely comfortable and their spindly lines take up less space than more conventional upholstered seats. They are brightened with a smart coat of white gloss. The chintz cushions are also predominantly white, printed with a riot of English garden flowers and piped in sapphire blue with tie-on bows. In a corner a jumble of cushions on which to sit and read pick up the colour scheme afresh – pink, white, blue – and the once sombre grandfather clock is transformed with a lick of whitewash into a slightly surreal object. White is used everywhere to pick up and enliven detail. A froth of white lace adds charm to the tea table, laid with sparsely sprigged white china. A floor of bare boards has been given a single coat of whitewash to provide a light-reflecting ground and introduce a sense of space. Everywhere a light, bright, holiday atmosphere predominates, heightened by summer flowers.

The challenge of decorating a modern house often lies in trying to maximize living space. In this spanking new London house, a solution was found using dynamic colour, graphic pattern, and a minimal approach to furniture.

Downstairs, one room serves as both sitting and dining area. The whole space was painted matt white and the floor given a distinctive, glossy surface of ceramic tiles. They give a cool, sharp finish to the room, which is divided into two areas by a boldly patterned Oriental rug. The same furnishing fabric was used throughout to integrate the scheme – a dominant pattern of deckchair stripes in tropical green and bright denim blue. Ordinary wooden kitchen chairs are given a slim, streamlined shape by their concealing covers.

In the dining area, a fold-flat chipboard table has a floor-length poppy red cloth with a graphic fabric flung over the top. A simple bench, fitting flush into the corner, takes up far less space than chairs, and looks sleeker. The door and windows are spruced with deckchair-striped curtains and pictures, framed in steel, pick up the poppy red theme. The lamp in the corner is a minimal upturned triangle on a black steel pole. Along the skirting board a paper border of black diamonds echoes the floor tiles and the same technique is applied to stunning effect in the hall, showing what can be done with just three decorative elements – white paint, black and white tiles, and a geometric border.

Emptying a room of colour is just as extreme an idea as flooding it with clashing primaries, but the result is calm, composed and easy to live with. Beige, that most chic of colours, warmer than white and less draining than grey, brings a softness to the hard, chill edge of northern daylight, and a sense of expansiveness to a small room.

Subtle gradations of colour prevent monotone from becoming monotonous: honey, buttermilk, blonde, ivory, cream and beige all intermingle with woodwork highlighted in white. The background is a neutral, wide-striped wallpaper, used in both the sitting area and above the wall cupboards in the kitchen. This kitchen recess can be hidden behind a freestanding screen when not in use. The chintz curtains are one of the room's most outstanding features; luxurious in length, their smooth, shiny texture looks completely contemporary. Chintz also covers the cushions, the edges of which are softened with the modernist's equivalent of a frill.

All is muted. The table and chairs have unusual covers with sharp arrows of inverted pleats and borders in slightly darker shades. The chairs are covered in the same natural undyed fabric as the sofa. In the compact kitchen, cream tiles and cupboards with pale, natural wood detail carry the unobtrusive theme through. Vases, lampstand, stools and bowls all take on a pleasing sense of this blueprint of 'the modern room'.

One of the hallmarks of modern style is a sensitivity to period features and the ability to create a modern room which heightens rather than negates them. This drawing room in a Berkshire house is a case in point, its restrained eighteenth-century panelling and lofty proportions quietly accentuated. Even the fine, grey marble fireplace fits the mood.

Soft, pale colours are used to create a muted background. The walls are washed with apricot and the panelling enhanced with apricot-tinged cream. The simplicity of combining two complementary colours – apricot and aquamarine – is used in both the other main features of the room: the curtains and the upholstery. Orange and pink may sound a jarring combination, but when the tone is right, unexpected colours can often work beautifully together. Here, the soft rose pink, deepened to Chinese plum blossom on the carpet, brings out the delicate warmth of the apricot and underpins the summery coolness of aquamarine. Some cushions are in a light sprig and trellis cotton with occasional larger blooms, but there is very little pattern in the room, one of the keys to its modern feel. Other decorative elements introduce different tones of the three colours, another very modern approach: the picture above the fireplace, the lacquer screen, the lampshade, rug and china dishes. It is the drawing out of serene colour which emphasizes the quality of light and gives the room its peaceful atmosphere.

A boy's room can be one of the most difficult rooms to decorate. While there are endless charming options for girls' rooms, boys seem more wary of 'decoration' altogether, and all too often this means they are left with an uninteresting box, meagrely decorated. What they need is a living space that emulates the energetic simplicity of their heroes, and in fact a hero or a hobby can spark off an original theme which gives character to a whole room. This fresh bedroom gets its ambience from a passion for the sea. The nautical theme is used not only for decorative objects but also in the general treatment of the room. Everything is unified by the simplicity of a marine colour scheme of blue and white. An unobtrusive border of stencilled leaves helps to lower the room to more cabin-like proportions.

Broad areas of white give a breezy outdoors feel. Floorboards take a gleaming coat of white satin gloss, above which the skirting is sapphire blue. Doors are painted blue with solid white panels. Recessed open shelves imitate the clever neatness of stowage space on board ship. The box bed in particular has a cabin-boy look to it, with its high sides. Bedlinen is lightly-striped, relieved by a blue clover-printed duvet and dominated by a splendid antique 'porthole' quilt. Both bed and chest of drawers are given a bleached, sea-worn sense of history with a blue paint finish.

Homework is done on a spartan school desk, but given an edge with a smart white-glossed chair with a deep denim blue cotton seat. This blue cotton is also used for a tablecloth, an armchair and Roman blinds. The armchair is a nice touch – children get an immense pleasure from having something so grown-up all to themselves. Decorative details relate mostly to the high seas down to a globe and a fishbowl, a ship's clock and even an old Noah's Ark.

Modern style is captured in this farmhouse bathroom by its bold approach to paint – the decoration message of this room, with its cheerful stripes of apricot and aquamarine. Paint colours are tied in with the Roman blind, which lends a streamlined look to the window and defines its shape, while the splashy pastel print of the cotton fabric has a youthful exuberance about it. A slick coat of white gloss paint enhances the floorboards, skirting, window frame and the old-fashioned radiator, adding a fresh, airy look to the room.

The bright, modern stripes of the walls were achieved by first painting the room with a wash of apricot. Then, using a plumb line to ensure the verticals were straight, the stripes were marked out using masking tape, and aquamarine paint was applied. The use of complementary tones ensures a subtle yet striking effect. The finishing touch is a lick of white paint for the 1930s Lloyd loom chair, and a cushion to match the blind.

LAURA ASHLEY SHOPS

AUSTRALIA

The Gallerie,
Gawler Place,
ADELAIDE,
South Australia 5000

1036 High Street,
ARMADALE,
Victoria,
Australia 3134

Shop 84,
Wintergarden,
171 Queen Street,
BRISBANE,
Queensland,
Australia 4000

Ship 58,
The Gallery,
Lemon Grove,
Victoria Avenue,
CHATSWOOD,
N.S.W.,
Australia 2067

3 Transvaal Avenue,
DOUBLE BAY,
N.S.W.,
Australia 2028

Shop 49,
Market Square,
Moorabool Street,
GEELONG,
Victoria,
Australia 3220

Centrepoint,
209 Murray Street,
HOBART,
Tasmania 7000

179 Collins Street,
MELBOURNE,
Victoria,
Australia 3000

City Arcade,
Hay Street Level,
PERTH,
Western Australia 6000

114 Castlereagh Street,
SYDNEY,
Australia

Mezzanine Level –
Centrepoint,
Castlereagh Street,
SYDNEY,
Australia

AUSTRIA

Judengasse 11,
SALZBURG

Weinburgasse 5,
1010 VIENNA

BELGIUM

Frankrijklei 27,
2000 ANTWERP

Le Grand Sablon 31,
1000 BRUSSELS
(Decorator Showroom)

CANADA

Sherway Gardens,
ETOBICOKE,
Ontario,
M9C 1B2

2110 Crescent Street,
MONTREAL,
Quebec,
H3G 2B8

136 Bank Street,
OTTAWA,
Ontario,
K1P 5N8

2452 Wilfred Laurier Bld,
STE-FOY,
Quebec,
G1V 2L1

18 Hazelton Avenue,
TORONTO,
Ontario,
M5R 2E2

1171 Robson Street,
VANCOUVER,
British Columbia,
V6E 1B5

Bayview Village Shopping
Center,
2901 Bayview Avenue,
WILLOWDALE,
Ontario,
M2K 1E6

Mail order:
Laura Ashley,
5165 Sherbrook Street W.,
Suite 124,
MONTREAL,
Quebec,
H4A 1T6

FRANCE

4 Rue Joseph Cabassol,
13100 AIX EN PROVENCE

2 Place du Palais,
Porte Cailhau,
33000 BORDEAUX

Centre Commercial
'Grand Var',
Avenue de l'Université,
83160 LA VALETTE
(Au Printemps)

Niveau 1,
Centre Commercial Parly 2,
Avenue Charles de Gaulle,
78150 LE CHESNAY
(Au Printemps)

Rez de Chaussée,
39–45 Rue Nationale,
59800 LILLE
(Au Printemps)

98 Rue Président Edouard
Herriot,
69002 LYON

2 ième Etage,
6 Avenue Jean Medicin,
0600 NICE

1er Etage,
40 Bld Haussmann,
75009 PARIS
(Galeries Lafayette)
Clothes only

5 ième Etage,
40 Bld Haussmann,
75009 PARIS
(Galeries Lafayette)
Home Furnishings

Le Printemps de la Mason,
7 ième Etage,
64 Bld Haussmann,
75009 PARIS

95 Avenue Raymond Poincaré,
75016 PARIS

94 Rue de Rennes,
75006 PARIS

261 Rue Saint Honoré,
75001 PARIS

34 Rue de Grenelle,
75007 PARIS

5 ième Etage,
1–5 Rue de la Haute Montée,
67004 STRASBOURG CEDEX

2 Rue du Temple Neuf,
67000 STRASBOURG

50 Rue Boulbonne,
31000 TOULOUSE

Niveau 3,
Avenue de l'Europe,
Centre Commercial Velizy II,
78140 VELIZY VILLACOUBLAY
(Au Printemps)

ITALY

4 Via Brera,
20121 MILAN

IRELAND

60–61 Grafton Street,
DUBLIN

JAPAN

8–22 Hondori,
Naka-Ku,
HIROSHIMA-SHI

2–4–14 Honcho,
Kichijoji,
MUSASHINO-SHI

1–26–19 Jiugaoka,
Meguro-Ku,
TOKYO

NETHERLANDS

Leidestraat 7,
1017 NS AMSTERDAM

Bakkerstraat 17,
6811 EG ARNHEM

Demer 24A,
5611 AS EINDHOVEN

Papestraat 17,
2513 AV S-GRAVENHAGE

M. Brugstraat 8,
6211 GK MAASTRICHT

Lijnbaan 63,
3012 EL ROTTERDAM

Oude Gracht 141,
3511 AJ UTRECHT

SWITZERLAND

Stadhausgasse 18,
4051 BASEL

8 Rue Verdaine,
1204 GENEVA

Augustinergasse 21,
8001 ZURICH

Augustinergasse 42–44,
ZURICH

WEST GERMANY

Holzgraben 1–3,
AACHEN

Karlsstrasse 15,
8900 AUGSBURG

Im Kadewe,
Tauentzienstr 21–24,
1000 BERLIN 30

Niedernstrasse 14,
4800 BIELEFELD

Sogestrasse 54,
2800 BREMEN 4

Hohestrasse 160–168,
5000 COLOGNE

Hunsruckenstrasse 43,
4000 DUSSELDORF

Goethestrasse 3,
6000 FRANKFURT AM MAIN 1

Neuer Wall,
73–75, 2000 HAMBURG

Georgestrasse 36,
3000 HANNOVER

Kaiserstrasse 187,
7500 KARKSTUHE

Ludgeriestrasse 79,
4400 MUENSTER

Sendlingerstrasse 37,
8000 MUNICH

Ludwigplatz 7,
3500 NUERNBERG

Breite Strasse 2,
700 STUTTGART 1

Langgasse,
6200 WIESBADEN

UNITED KINGDOM

191–197 Union Street,
ABERDEEN

10 Hale Leys,
AYLESBURY

The Bear Inn,
Market Place,
BANBURY

Winchester Road,
BASINGSTOKE
(Sainsbury's Homebase)

The Old Red House,
8–9 New Bond Street,
BATH

Pines Way,
BATH
(Sainsbury's Homebase)

75 High Street,
BEDFORD

14–16 Priory,
Queensway,
BIRMINGHAM

147 New Street,
BIRMINGHAM
Clothes only

80 Old Christchurch Road,
BOURNEMOUTH

762 Harrogate Road,
BRADFORD
(Sainsbury's Homebase)

Ashley Road,
Parkstone,
Poole
BRANKSOME,
(Sainsbury's Homebase)

45 East Street,
BRIGHTON

62 Queens Road,
Clifton,
BRISTOL

39 Broadmead,
BRISTOL

1 The Lexicon Cornhill,
BURY ST EDMUNDS

14 Trinity Street,
CAMBRIDGE

41–42 Burgate,
CANTERBURY

5 High Street,
CARDIFF

Colchester Avenue,
off Newport Road,
Roath,
CARDIFF
(Sainsbury's Homebase)

3–4 Grapes Lane,
CARLISLE

10–13 Grays Brewery Yard,
Springfield Road,
CHELMSFORD

100 The Promenade,
CHELTENHAM

17–19 Watergate Row,
CHESTER

32 North Street,
CHICHESTER

1 Trinity Square,
CHICHESTER

St Andrews Avenue,
COLCHESTER
(Sainsbury's Homebase)

Junction Fletchampstead
Highway & Sir Henry
Parks Road,
COVENTRY
(Sainsbury's Homebase)

Stadium Way,
CRAYFORD
(Sainsbury's Homebase)

8 Albert Street,
DERBY

129–131 Terminus Road,
EASTBOURNE

137 George Street,
EDINBURGH

126 Princes Street,
EDINBURGH

41–42 High Street,
EXETER

The Barn,
Lion & Lamb Yard,
FARNHAM

Metro Centre,
GATESHEAD

84–90 Buchanan Street,
GLASGOW

215 Sauchiehall Street,
GLASGOW

St Oswalds Road,
GLOUCESTER
(Sainsbury's Homebase)

Old Cloth Hall,
North Street,
GUILDFORD

3–5 James Street,
HARROGATE

3–4 Middle Street,
HORSHAM

Priory Sidings,
Sainsbury Way,
Hesle Road,
Hessle,
HULL
(Sainsbury's Homebase)

Felixstowe Road,
IPSWICH
(Sainsbury's Homebase)

17 Buttermarket,
IPSWICH

108 The Parade,
LEAMINGTON SPA

Church Institute,
9 Lands Lane,
LEEDS

King Lane,
Moortown,
LEEDS
(Sainsbury's Homebase)

6 Eastgate,
LEICESTER
(Sainsbury's Homebase)

19–23 Cavern Walks,
Matthew Street,
LIVERPOOL

30 Great Oak Street,
LLANIDLOES

LONDON:

256–258 Regent Street,
Oxford Circus,
LONDON W1

35–36 Bow Street,
LONDON WC2

7–9 Harriet Street,
LONDON SW1

71–73 Lower Sloane Street,
LONDON SW1
(Decorator Showroom)

157 Fulham Road,
LONDON SW3

D6/V13 Brent Cross Shopping
Centre,
BRENT CROSS,
London NW4

90–92 High Street,
BROMLEY

10 Beckenham Hills Road,
CATFORD,
London SE6
(Sainsbury's Homebase)

11 Drummond Place,
CROYDON

66A Purley Way,
CROYDON
(Sainsbury's Homebase)

Unit 17,
Waterglade Centre,
EALING,
London W5

36–37 High Street,
HAMPSTEAD,
London NW3

Rookery Way,
The Hyde,
HENDON,
London NW9
(Sainsbury's Homebase)

714–720 High Road,
Seven Kings,
ILFORD
(Sainsbury's Homebase)

Macmillan House,
The Old Town Hall,
KENSINGTON,
London W8

32–33 Market Place,
KINGSTON-UPON-THAMES

229–253 Kingston Road,
NEW MALDEN
(Sainsbury's Homebase)

3 Station road,
NEW SOUTHGATE,
London W8
(Sainsbury's Homebase)

45 Oakfield Road,
off Penge High Street,
PENGE,
London SE20
(Sainsbury's Homebase)

68 George Street,
RICHMOND

3–4 Times Square,
SUTTON

2c Fulborne Road,
WALTHAMSTOW,
London E17
(Sainsbury's Homebase)

473 High Street,
WILLESDEN,
London NW10
(Sainsbury's Homebase)

8–10 King Street,
MAIDSTONE

28 King Street,
MANCHESTER

48 Linthorpe Road,
MIDDLESBROUGH

40–42 Midsummer Arcade,
MILTON KEYNES

45 High Street,
NEWCASTLE-UNDER-LYME

8 Nelson Street,
NEWCASTLE-UPON-TYNE

Victoria Promenade,
NORTHAMPTON
(Sainsbury's Homebase)

19 London Street,
NORWICH

58 Bridlesmith Gate,
NOTTINGHAM

Castle Marina Park,
Castle Boulevard,
NOTTINGHAM
(Sainsbury's Homebase)

50 Halesowen Street,
OLDBURY
(Sainsbury's Homebase)

26–27 Cornmarket,
OXFORD

26–27 Little Clarendon Street,
OXFORD

189–191 High Street,
PERTH

Unit 90,
Queensgate Centre,
PETERBOROUGH

The Armada Centre,
PLYMOUTH

Claydon's Lane,
RAYLEIGH WEIR
(Sainsbury's Homebase)

75–76 Broad Street,
READING

50 Kenavon Drive,
READING
(Sainsbury's Homebase)

13 Market Place,
ST ALBANS

49–51 New Canal,
SALISBURY

87 Pinstone Street,
SHEFFIELD

65 Wyle Cop,
SHREWSBURY

2 Above Bar Church,
High Street,
SOUTHAMPTON

Lordshill Shopping Centre,
SOUTHAMPTON
(Sainsbury's Homebase)

107 High Street,
SOUTHEND

465–467 Lord Street,
SOUTHPORT

41–42 Henley Street,
STRATFORD-UPON-AVON

Unit 4, 164 The Parade,
Grace Church Centre,
SUTTON COLDFIELD

Quay Parade,
SWANSEA
(Sainsbury's Homebase)

19E Regent Street,
SWINDON

2–4 High Street,
TAUNTON

19–21 High Street,
TENTERDEN

61 Calverley Road,
TUNBRIDGE WELLS

Ing's Road,
WAKEFIELD
(Sainsbury's Homebase)

Junction Bradford &
Midland Road,
WALSALL
(Sainsbury's Homebase)

Sturlas Way,
WALTHAM CROSS
(Sainsbury's Homebase)

50 Halesowen Street,
WARLEY
West Midlands

Unit 3,
1–7 The Parade,
High Street,
WATFORD

114 St Albans Road,
WATFORD
(Sainsbury's Homebase)

17 Grove Street,
WILMSLOW

10 The Square,
WINCHESTER

32 Peascod Street,
WINDSOR

Crown Passage,
Broad Street,
WORCESTER

Hylton Road,
WORCESTER
(Sainsbury's Homebase)

Unit 28,
Vicarage Walk,
Quedam Centre,
YEOVIL

7 Daveygate,
YORK

Junction Monkgate/Foss Bank,
YORK
(Sainsbury's Homebase)

UNITED STATES

Crossgates Mall,
120 Washington Avenue
Extension,
ALBANY, NY 12203

139 Main Street,
ANNAPOLIS, MD 21401

514 East Washington Street,
ANN ARBOR, MI 48104

29 Surburban Square,
ARDMORE, PA 19003

Lenox Square,
3393 Peachtree Road,
ATLANTA, GA 30326

Perimeter Mall,
4400 Ashford-Dunwoody
Road,
ATLANTA, GA 30346

Highland Mall 1224,
6001 Airport Boulevard,
AUSTIN, TX 78752

Pratt Street Pavilion,
Harborplace,
BALTIMORE, MD 21202

203 Beachwood Place,
26300 Cedar Road,
BEACHWOOD, OH 44122

200–219 Riverchase
Galleria Mall,
BIRMINGHAM, AL 35244

180 Town Center Mall,
BOCA RATON, FL 33431

83 Newbury Street,
BOSTON, MA 02116

23 Church Street,
BURLINGTON, VT 05401

Charles Square,
5 Bennett Street,
CAMBRIDGE, MA 02138

Carmel Plaza,
CARMEL-BY-THE-SEA,
CA 93921

Charleston Place,
130 Market Street,
CHARLESTON, SC 29401

The Mall at Chesnut Hill,
199 Boylston Street,
CHESNUT HILL, MA 02167

Watertower Place,
835 N. Michigan Avenue,
CHICAGO, IL 60611

The Citadel,
750 Citadel Drive E. 2008,
COLORADO SPRINGS,
CO 80909

1636 Redwood Highway,
CORTE MADERA,
CA 94925

3333 Bristol Street,
South Coast Plaza,
COSTA MESA, CA 92629

Galleria 13350 Dallas Parkway,
Suite 1585,
DALLAS, TX 75240

423 North Park Center,
DALLAS, TX 75225

Danbury Fair Mall C-118,
7 Backus Avenue,
DANBURY,
CT 06810

1439 Larimer Street,
DENVER, CO 80202

The Kaleidoscope at the Hub,
555 Walnut Street,
Suite 218,
DES MOINES, IA 50309

Twelve Oaks Mall,
27498 Novi Road,
Suite A,
DETROIT, MI 48056

Galleria Shopping center,
3505 West 69th Street,
EDINA, MN 55435

11822 Fair Oaks Mall,
FAIRFAX, VA 22033

West Farms Mall,
FARMINGTON, CT 06032

2492 E. Sunrise Boulevard,
Galleria Mall,
FORT LAUDERDALE,
FL 33304

213 Hulen Mall,
FORT WORTH, TX 76132

58 Main Street,
FREEPORT, ME 04032

Saddle Creek Shopping Center,
7615 W. Farmington
Boulevard,
GERMANTON,
TN 38138

Glendale Galleria,
GLENDALE, CA 91210

Woodland Mall,
3175 28th Street S.E.,
GRAND RAPIDS, MI 49508

321 Greenwich Avenue,
GREENWICH, CT 06830

Riverside Square Mall,
HACKENSACK, NJ 07601

Ala Moana Center 2246,
HONOLULU, HI 96814

The Galleria,
5015 Westheimer,
Suite 2120,
HOUSTON, TX 77056

1000 West Oaks Mall,
Suite 124,
HOUSTON, TX 77082

Fashion Mall,
8702 Keystone Crossing,
INDIANAPOLIS, IN 46240

The Jacksonville Landing,
2 Independent Drive,
JACKSONVILLE, FL 32202

Country Club Plaza,
308 W. 47th Street,
KANSAS CITY,
MO 64112

The Esplanade,
1401 W. Esplanade,
KENNER, LA 70065

White Flint Shopping Mall,
11301 Rockville Pike,
KENSINGSTON, MD 20895

7852 Girard Avenue,
LA JOLLA, CA 92037

Pavilion in the Park,
8201 Cantrell Road,
LITTLE ROCK, AR 72207

10250 Santa Monica Boulevard,
LOS ANGELES, CA 90067

Beverly Center,
121 N. La Cienaga Boulevard,
Suite 739,
LOS ANGELES, CA 90048

Louisville Galleria 109,
LOUISVILLE, KY 40202

2042 Northern Boulevard,
Americana Shopping Center,
MANHASSET, NY 11030

Tysons Corner Center,
1961 Chain Bridge Road,
MCLEAN, VA 22102

The Falls,
Space 373,
8888 Howard Drive,
MIAMI, FL 33176

The Grand Avenue,
275 W. Wisconsin Avenue 5,
MILWAUKEE, WI 53203

208 City Center,
40 South 7th Street,
MINNEAPOLIS, MN 55402

Ridgedale Center,
12401 Wayzota Boulevard,
MINNETONKA, MN 55343

The Mall at Green Hills,
2148 Abbot Martin Road,
NASHVILLE, TN 37215

260–262 College Street,
NEW HAVEN, CT 06510

333 Canal Street,
151 Canal Place,
NEW ORLEANS,
LA 70130

714 Madison Avenue,
NEW YORK,
NY 10021
(Decorator Showroom)

398 Columbus Avenue,
NEW YORK,
NY 10024

4 Fulton Street,
NEW YORK, NY 10038

21 East 57th Street,
NEW YORK, NY 10021

2164 Northbrook Court,
NORTHBROOK, IL 60062

224 Oakbrook Center,
OAKBROOK, IL 60521

Owings Mills Town Center,
10300 Mill Run Circle 1062,
OWINGS MILLS,
MD 21117

320 Worth Avenue,
PALM BEACH,
FL 33480

469 Desert Fashion Plaza,
123 North Palm Canyon Drive,
PALM SPRINGS, CA 92262

12 Stanford Shopping Center,
PALO ALTO, CA 94304

221 Paramus Park,
Route 17,
PARAMUS, NJ 07652

401 South Lake Avenue,
PASADENA, CA 91101

1721 Walnut Street,
PHILADELPHIA,
PA 19103

Biltmore Fashion Park,
2478 E. Camelback Road,
PHOENIX, AZ 85016

20 Commerce Court,
Station Square,
PITTSBURGH, PA 15219

1000 Ross Park Mall,
PITTSBURGH,
PA 15237

2100 Collin Creek Mall,
811 No. Central Expressway,
PLANO, TX 75075

419 S.W. Morrison Street,
PORTLAND, OR 97204

46 Nassau Street,
Palmer Square,
PRINCETON,
NJ 08544

2 Davol Square Mall,
Point & Eddy Street,
PROVIDENCE,
RI 02903

Crabtree Valley Mall,
4325 Glenwood Avenue,
RALEIGH,
NC 27612

South Bay Galleria,
1815 Hawthorne Boulevard,
Space 172,
REDONDO BEACH,
CA 90278

Commercial Block,
1217 E. Cary Street,
RICHMOND,
VA 23219

Regency Square Mall,
1404 Parham Road,
RICHMOND, VA 23229

Northpark Mall,
1200 East County Line Road,
RIDGELAND, MI 39157

531 Pavilions Lane,
SACRAMENTO, CA 95825

74 Plaza Frontenac,
ST LOUIS, MO 63131

St Louis Center C-330
515 N. 6th Street,
ST LOUIS, MO 63101

Trolley Square,
SALT LAKE CITY, UT 84102

247 Horton Plaza,
Space 265,
SAN DIEGO, CA 92101

University Town Center,
SAN DIEGO, CA 92122

1827 Union Street,
SAN FRANCISCO, CA 94123

563 Sutter Street,
SAN FRANCISCO, CA 94102
(Decorator Showroom)

Suite 1224,
North Star Mall,
7400 SAN PEDRO,
San Antonio, TX 78216

Le Cumba Galleria,
3891 State Street 109,
SANTA BARBARA, CA 93105

Valley Fair Mall,
Suite 1031,
2855 Stevens Creek Boulevard,
SANTA CLARA, CA 95050

696 White Plains Road,
SCARSDALE,
NY 10583

F-331 Woodfield Mall,
SCHAUMBURG, IL 60173

405 University Street,
SEATTLE, DC 98101

The Mall at Short Hills,
SHORT HILLS, NJ 07078

20 Old Orchard Shopping
Center,
SKOKIE, IL 60077

Stamford Town Center,
100 Greyrock Place,
STAMFORD. CT 06902

139 Main Street,
STONY BROOK, NY 11790

Old Hyde Park Village,
718 S. Village Circle,
TAMPA, FL 33606

2845 Somerset Mall,
TROY, MI 48084

Utica Square,
1846 21 Street,
TULSA, OK 74114

1171 Broadway Plaza,
WALNUT CREEK, CA 94596

3213 M. Street NW,
Georgetown,
WASHINGTON, DC 20007

85 Main Street,
WESTPORT, CT 06880

Bullocks Westwood Shops,
10861 Weyburn Avenue,
WESTWOOD, CA 90025

422 Duke of Gloucester Street,
WILLIAMSBURG, VA 23185

290 Park Avenue North,
WINTER PARK,
Florida 32789

740 Hanes Mall,
WINSTON-SALEM, NC 27103

279 Promenade Mall,
WOODLAND HILLS, CA 91367

108 Worthington Square Mall,
WORTHINGTON, OH 43085

Mail order:

Laura Ashley Inc.,
1300 MacArthur Boulevard,
MAHWAH, NJ 07430

STOCKISTS

18 Ioannou Metaxa Street,
Glyfada,
ATHENS,
Greece

28 Herodotou Street,
10673 Kolonaki,
ATHENS,
Greece

Engen 51,
5000 BERGEN,
Norway

P.O. Box 7910,
Sheikh Rashid Building,
Zabeel Road,
DUBAI,
United Arab Emirates

29 Wyndham Street,
Central,
HONG KONG

Riddervoldsgate 10B,
OSLO 2,
Norway

De Gruchys,
King Street,
ST HELIER,
Jersey

36 Le Bordage,
ST PETER PORT,
Guernsey

300–301 Eachon-Dong,
Yongssan-Kij,
SEOUL,
South Korea

Yliopistonkatu 33,
SF–20100 TURKU 10,
Finland

BIBLIOGRAPHY

Aslet, Clive, *The Last Country Houses*, Yale 1982
Bel Geddes, Norman, *Horizons*, Little, Brown 1932
Campbell, Colen, *Vitruvius Britannicus*, 1715
Chambers, Sir William, *Treatise on Civil Architecture*, 1759
Clark, Sir Kenneth, *The Gothic Revival*, Constable 1928
Cornforth, John, *The Inspiration of the Past*, Viking 1985
Fowler, John and Cornforth, John, *English Decoration in the Eighteenth Century*,
    Barrie and Jenkins 1974
Fry, Roger, *Letters* Ed. Denys Sutton, Chatto and Windus 1972
Girouard, Mark, *Life in the English Country House*, Yale 1978
Harcourt Smith, Simon, *The Last of Uptake*, Batsford 1983
Hillier, Bevis, *The Style of the Century*, Dutton 1983
Hoggart, Richard, *The Uses of Literacy*, Chatto and Windus 1957
Hope, Thomas, *Household Furniture and Interior Decoration*, 1807
Huysman, J. K., *A Rebours*, 1884
Jones, Owen, *The Grammar of Ornament*, 1956; reprint
    Studio Editions 1986
Jourdain, Margaret, *English Interior Decoration 1500–1830 : A Study in the
    Development of Design*, Batsford 1950
Lancaster, Osbert, *Pillar to Post*, John Murray 1938

Larsson, Carl, *The House in the Sun*, 1904
Le Corbusier, *Manual of the Dwelling*, 1923
Morphet, Richard, 'The Significance of Charleston', *Apollo* November 1976
Muthesius, Herman, *The English House*, 1904
Nelson, George, *Tomorrow's House*, 1950
Palladio, Andrea, *I quattro libri dell'architettura*, 1715
Ramsay, Stanley C. and Harvey, J. D. M., *Small Georgian Houses and their Details,
    1750–1820*, Architectural Press 1972
Robinson, John Martin, *The Latest Country Houses*, Bodley Head 1984
Ruskin, John, *Modern Painters*, Smith & Elder 1846
Rykwert, Joseph and Anne, *The Brothers Adam*, Collins 1984
Snodin, Michael and others, *Rococo*, Trefoil 1984
Spalding, Frances, *Vanessa Bell*, Weidenfeld & Nicolson 1983
Steegman, John, *The Rule of Taste*, Macmillan 1936
Thornton, Peter, *Authentic Decor*, Weidenfeld & Nicolson 1986
Waugh, Evelyn, *A Handful of Dust*, Chatman & Hall 1934
Waugh, Evelyn, *Brideshead Revisited*, Chatman & Hall 1945
Wharton, Edith and Ogden Codman, *The Decoration of Houses*, New York 1897
Whistler, Laurence, *The Laughter and the Urn, the life of Rex Whistler*, Weidenfeld
    & Nicolson 1986

ACKNOWLEDGMENTS

All pictures are reproduced courtesy of the Laura Ashley Archives, with the exception of the following:

PAGE

14 Henry Sylvester Stannard, *Sailing the Boat*
Fine Art Photographic Library

15 S. Hayllar, *May Day*
Fine Art Photographic Library

16 W. Ackerman, George IV's Cottage at Windsor Great Park
Windsor Castle Royal Library, Her Majesty the Queen

17 Sir John Soane's design for a Dairy
Victoria and Albert Museum, London (photo Angelo Hornak)

18 Frederick Daniel Hardy, *The Foreign Guest*
Fine Art Photographic Library

19 Nineteenth-century sampler
Norfolk Museums Service (Strangers' Hall Museum, Norwich)

20 William Morris wallpaper design: Jasmine Trellis
Victoria and Albert Museum, London (Weidenfeld & Nicolson Archives)

21 T. M. Rooke, Burne-Jones's London Dining Room
Mary Ryde (Weidenfeld & Nicolson Archives)

22 Walter Crane, frontispiece to *The House Beautiful*, 1896
Victoria and Albert Museum, London (Bridgeman Art Library)

23 Charles Voysey fabric design, printed by G. P. and J. Baker Ltd
Victoria and Albert Museum, London (Bridgeman Art Library)

24 ABOVE LEFT Carl Larsson, *Brita's Forty Winks* from the series *At Home*
National Museum, Stockholm (photo Statens Konstmuseer)

ABOVE RIGHT M. Grösser, A Viennese Drawing Room
Historisches Museum der Stadt Wien, Vienna

BELOW Nineteenth-century painted chair, Pennsylvania
The American Museum in Britain, Bath

25 ABOVE Cover of *The Craftsman*, vol. V, January 1904
Victoria and Albert Museum, London (Weidenfeld & Nicolson Archives/photo Eileen Tweedy)

BELOW Baltimore Bridal Quilt
The American Museum in Britain, Bath

26 ABOVE and BELOW From The Studio's *Year Book of Decorative Art*, 1919

27 Waring and Gillow kitchen design from *The Book of the Home*, vol. II, ed. Mrs C. E. Humphry, first published 1914

50 Eighteenth-century sampler Royal Scottish Museum, Edinburgh

51 LEFT Grinling Gibbons, Carved panel from Petworth House, Sussex
Weidenfeld & Nicolson Archives

RIGHT David Cox, Hardwick Hall: The Long Gallery
Trustees of the Chatsworth Estate (photo Angelo Hornak)

52 Johann Zoffany, *Queen Charlotte in her Dressing Room in Buckingham House*
Reproduced by gracious permission of Her Majesty the Queen

PAGE

54 ABOVE A. Sebriako, Ditchley Park, Oxfordshire; designed by William Kent ET Archive

BELOW John Venn, Architectural section through an eighteenth-century house, 1774
The Royal Academy of Arts, London

55 ABOVE Robert Adam, Design for the ceiling of the Fishing House, Kedleston Hall, Derbyshire, *c.* 1769
Courtesy of the Kedleston Hall Appeal/The National Trust

BELOW Robert Adam, Design for one wall of a Book Room, Kedleston Hall, Derbyshire, 1768
Courtesy of the Kedleston Hall Appeal/The National Trust

56 ABOVE John Nash, Views of the Royal Pavilion, Brighton: The Corridor in 1815
Photo Angelo Hornak

BELOW Drawn by C. Wild, engraved by R. Reeve, *The Blue Velvet Closet*, Carlton House, London
Guildhall Library, London (Bridgeman Art Library)

58 W. H. Bartlett, *The Boudoir, The Deepdene, Surrey*, a Thomas Hope design
Lambeth Archives Department (photo M. D. Trace)

59 ABOVE Knighthayes, the north front, *c.* 1867
The National Trust

BELOW Nineteenth-century paisley shawl
Victoria and Albert Museum, London

60 From *Interior Woodwork*, *c.* 1910, a Neo-Georgian design
Victoria and Albert Museum, London

61 From Ernest Foussier's *Nouveaux Modèles de Tentures, Décorations de Fenêtres*, Paris, 1900
Victoria and Albert Museum, London

84 John Edward, Anemones from *A Collection of Flowers drawn after Nature*, 1783–85 Weidenfeld & Nicolson Archives

85 Samuel Rayner, Bedroom in a Town House, *c.* 1855
Weidenfeld & Nicolson Archives

86 ABOVE The Green Closet, Ham House, Surrey
Victoria and Albert Museum, London

BELOW Schloss Nymphenburg, nr Munich, The Grand Salon designed by François Cuviliés, 1739
Photo Angelo Hornak

87 ABOVE Antoine Watteau, *La Gamme d'Amour*
The National Gallery, London

BELOW Design for a brocaded damask, 1744
Victoria and Albert Museum, London

88 John Carter, *The Holbein Chamber at Strawberry Hill*, from Horace Walpole's *A Description of the Villa, 1784*
Courtesy of the Lewis Walpole Library, Yale University

89 LEFT A Gothic-style Window Seat Photo Fritz von der Schulenburg

INDEX

Page numbers in *italics* refer to captions